People's Representatives
Theory and Practice of Parliamentary Democracy in Tanzania

Editors

Rwekaza S. Mukandala
Samuel S. Mushi
Casmir Rubagumya

Fountain Publishers

Fountain Publishers Ltd
P.O. Box 488 Kampala
E-mail:fountain@starcom.co.ug
Website:www.fountainpublishers.com

© Research and Education for Developement in Tanzania 2004
First published 2004

All rights reserved. No part of this publication may be reproduced, stored in a retrieval system or transmitted in any form or by any means electronic, mechanical, photocopying, recording or otherwise without the prior written permission of the publisher.

ISBN 9970 02 438 8

Cataloguing-in-Publication Data
– p; – cm.
Peoples' representatives: theory and practice of parliamentary democracy in Tanzania/edited by Rwekaza S. Mukandala, Samuel S. Mushi, Casmir Rubagumya – Kampala: Fountain Publishers, 2004.

ISBN 9970 02 438 8
1. Democracy – Tanzania   I. Mukandala, Rwekaza S.
II. Mushi, Samuel S. III. Rubagumya Casmir

   321.409678

Contents

1. Introduction — 1
   Rwekaza S. Mukandala

2. Methodology — 7
   Deogratias Rugaimukamu

3. Historical and Theoretical Analysis of Representation — 25
   Samuel S. Mushi

4. The ups and downs of the Tanzanian Parliament 1961-1994 — 46
   Kapwepwe I. Tambila

5. The General Environment in which the Members of Parliament Works — 73
   Charles Gasarasi

6. The Role of Members of Parliament as Representatives of the People — 93
   Athumani Liviga

7. The Relationship of Members of Parliament with other Political Actors: Government, Own Party and Voters — 113
   Ernest T. Mallya

8. Lobbying the Parliament in Tanzania: Structures and Processes — 134
   Amon E. Chaligha

9. The Political Competence of Voters and their Members of Parliament — 166
   Amos Mhina

10. Comparing Performances: The 1990-1995 Single-Party Parliament and the 1995-2000 Multi-party Parliament — 183
    Bernadeta Killian

    Index — 201

Acronyms

AG	–	Attorney General
ASP	–	Afro-Shiraze Party
ATE	–	The Tanzania Employers Association
CCM	–	Chama Cha Mapinduzi
CHADEMA	–	Chama Cha Demokrasia na Maendeleo
CTI	–	The Confederation of Tanzanian Industries
CUF	–	Civic United Front
DPP	–	Director of Public Persecutions
ESRF	–	The Economic and Social Research Foundation
FES	–	The Friedrich Ebert Stiftung Foundation
G-55	–	Group of 55 Members of Parliament who pressed for the motion of revival of the government of Tanganyika
H/KK	–	Hakuna/kakata kutoa jibu
ILO	–	The International Labour Organisation
LEGCO	–	Legislative Council
MP	–	Member of Parliament
NCCR	–	National Convention for Construction and Reform
NCCR-M	–	National Convention for Construction and Reform – Mageuzi
NEC	–	The National Executive Committee
NGOs	–	Non-governmental Organisations
OIC	–	The Organisation of Islamic Community
OTTU	–	The Organisation of Tanzania's Trade Union.
PAC	–	The Public Accounts Committee
REDET	–	Research and Education for Democracy in Tanzania
SPSS	–	The Statistical Package and Software Systems
TANU	–	The Tanganyiks African National Union

TCC/A	–	The Tanzanian Chamber of Commerce, Industry and Agriculture
TEMCO	–	Tanzania Electoral Monitoring Commission
TFTU	–	The Tanzania Federation of Free Trade Union
UDP	–	United Democratic Party
URT	–	United Republic of Tanzania
UWT	–	Umoja wa Wanawake Tanzania

1

Introduction

Rwekaza S. Mukandala

Parliament is a very critical institution in any democratic political system. Together with the executive and judiciary it completes an ensemble of institutions whose balanced existence and functioning ensures that decisions are reached democratically and legitimately and executed efficiently and effectively. Parliament performs many important functions in a democratic polity. Historically, African parliaments have been instruments of liberation. As Ali Mazrui argues, nationalist movements demanded representation on the Colonial Legislative Council (LEGCO). As shown by K.I. Tambila in this book, two chiefs were appointed to Tanganyika's LEGCO in November 1945. Success in the struggle for independence was reflected in the changing and expanding composition of the LEGCO as well as conditions for membership until it became the parliament of independent Tanganyika. Parliament has also continued to be an organ of liberation for women. Special seats have always been reserved for women in Tanzania's parliament. Act No. 4 of 1992 and Act No. 12 of 1995 increased the number of special seats for women from a fixed 15 seats to 15 per cent of all seats and later to no less than 20 per cent of all other members of parliament. Their number is now to progressively increase until they reach 30 per cent of all other Members of Parliament (MPs). It has also been argued that Tanzania's parliament has been an instrument of cultural liberation. Debates and other proceedings of parliament have been conducted in Kiswahili. This has made it possible for more Tanzanians who may have otherwise been inhibited by their weak command of the English language to aspire to be parliamentarians. In the final analysis, the use of Kiswahili has brought parliament closer to the people, serving to demystify both parliament and the entire political and policy making process, as ordinary people have been able to follow parliamentary proceedings.

Parliament has also been a platform for national debate. Apart from universities, parliament is the other arena where open and candid expression is expected, demanded and protected. The Parliamentary Immunities, Powers and Privileges Act, 1988, Sec. 3, states that 'There shall be freedom of speech and debate in the Assembly and such freedom of speech and debate shall not be liable to be questioned in any court or place outside the Assembly.'

Also, parliament through the use of votes of confidence and votes of censure can act as a check on the executive. According to Act. No. 2 of 1992, parliament has to endorse the appointment of the prime minister; ratify non-self-executing treatise (Act. 63/2e); can impeach the president or vice-President; holds ministers accountable; and through committees play a surveillance role on activities of government.

Finally, parliament plays an important function in the budgetary process. It passes the necessary legislation to levy taxes and authorise expenditure. It questions the various allocations of resources made by various ministries. Parliament can be an instrument of social control passing laws that influence and control behaviour, including crime and marriage. Parliament may spearhead reform passing legislation protecting the rights of women for example. Parliament also has a role in national policy formulation acting as a bridge between the judiciary and the executive.

Parliament can also play a negative role. Most legislatures in post-independent Africa played a rubber-stamp function endorsing even the most outrageous requests from the executive. The classic case but by no means the exception, is one involving Ugandan parliamentarians who on 15 April, 1966, abolished the 1962 Constitution and adopted a new one after being advised by the executive to 'go down to your pigeon holes for your copies of the new constitution.' Parliament can be a sponge on public resources. Parliamentarians can vote high salaries, hefty allowances and other fringe benefits for themselves while the executive in need of a pliant house looks the other way. Parliament can also encourage or condone corruption and would be parliamentarians turn multiparty competition into a cut-throat free-for-all where every means of competition including intrigue, bribery, rigging, etc is used. This study focuses on the Tanzanian Parliament.

Deogratias Rugaimukamu provides a detailed description of the methodology that was used in the study carried out in 1999, which is the source of most papers included in this volume. The chapter underlines the importance of careful planning of sample surveys at all stages: sampling, preparation of research instruments, data collection, data processing and analysis. Some of the problems that emerged during this exercise are briefly discussed.

In Chapter Three, Samuel Mushi sets the stage by analysing representation as it has evolved historically in Western Europe and North America. Among other things, the chapter outlines the main principles of representation in liberal democracies. It also discusses factors which can either facilitate or constrain representation. These factors can be economic, or can pertain to political structure or to political culture. Two representation models: the individualist model (US) and the collectivist model (UK) are discussed at some length. Finally, the main functions of the representative at three levels (national, constituency and personal) are outlined. This chapter gives a theoretical anchor to subsequent chapters in the volume. The research on the role of MPs in Tanzania was guided by historical and theoretical issues raised in this chapter.

The history of the Tanzanian Parliament from 1961 to 1994 is sketched by K.I. Tambila in Chapter Four. The highlights of this chapter underscore the point that there has always been struggle for supremacy between parliament and the executive arm of government. On attaining independence in 1961, Tanganyika inherited the Westminster model of government by which parliament was supreme. However, in 1962 when Tanganyika became a Republic the locus of power shifted from parliament to the presidency. Under the Interim Constitution of 1965, the powers of parliament were further eroded in favour of the executive and the ruling single party. Parliament was reduced to a rubber – stamping institution for decisions made by the party. Parliament started to gradually regain its lost powers in 1984, when the constitution was amended. These gains were further enhanced by the 1992 constitutional amendment which ushered in multiparty democracy. These gains notwithstanding, the author warns that the presidency is still a very powerful institution and that the executive and the judiciary are very corrupt. In these circumstances, parliament will find it very difficult to exercise its control functions.

In Chapter Five, C. Gasarasi surveys the general environment in which the Tanzanian Member of parliament works. He argues that under the one-party system, MPs were constrained in their work because of the all-powerful single party and executive branch of the government. With the advent of the multi-party system, the environment is more enabling. Several pieces of legislation have liberated MPs from the tight control of the executive. At the same time, MPs have more flexibility and autonomy in their actions. The author further argues that the environment in which MPs work is supportive in the sense that generally, MPs enjoy the support of both local and national government, their respective political parties, voters, and Non-governmental Organisations (NGOs). The working environment, on the other hand, is constrained by the individualistic motive of most MPs. When supposed peoples' representatives are motivated more by remuneration packages and less by civic duty, they are not likely to effectively discharge their duties. Similarly, the perceived lack of authority and power among MPs has a negative effect on their will to perform optimally. Creativity and initiative are therefore nipped in the bud. Another constraining factor in the MPs' working environment pointed out by the author is lack of staff and aides to do research, give expert advice to MPs on important policy issues, organise civic functions, etc.

In Chapter Six, Athumani Liviga argues that whereas voters believe they have the final say over their representatives, the MPs claim that their right to represent the voters stems from the constitution. This implies that they do not necessarily consider themselves responsible to the people who voted them into office. The author suggests that voters should be given the power to recall MPs who do not perform to the voters satisfaction. He also suggests that deliberate efforts must be made to educate voters and the general public on their civic rights and obligations.

In Chapter Seven, Ernest T. Mallya looks at the relationship between MPs as representatives of the people and three other actors: the government, the political parties to which they belong and their constituents. He argues that all the three actors play key role in the process of choosing the representatives of the people and in facilitating the job of MPs once elected. Voters have the power to vote MPs in or out office. While the government (both local and central) is the vehicle by which MPs can hope to deliver goods to their constituents. The author concludes that like everywhere in the world, representation in Tanzania is not perfect. He is however, optimistic that with time the process can be improved significantly.

Amon E. Chaligha discusses parliamentary lobbying in Tanzania in Chapter Eight. He points out that organised groups do lobby parliament, but this is done informally and haphazardly since there is no institutional framework for formal lobbying. In this state of affairs, the author argues, parliament often passes legislation which affects members of organised groups without consulting them. Further, he argues that MPs are disadvantaged because they do not always get expert information and advice concerning different bills tabled in parliament, a problem that formal lobbying would greatly reduce. The author makes several suggestions on procedural changes needed to make lobbying more systematic and more institutionalised.

In Chapter Nine, Amos Mhina looks at the political competence of voters and their members of parliament. He reveals that a significant number of MPs believe that their voters could summon them in case of poor performance. They disagree, however, with the proposition that voters should have the right to remove an MP whose performance is not satisfactory before the end of his or her five year term. On the other hand, voters think that the present constitution set up should be changed to give voters the right to sanction their MPs for poor performance or gross misconduct. The author concludes that the performance of MPs, both at constituency and national level, needs to be improved and that a new working relationship between MPs and their constituents needs to be established.

In the last Chapter, Bernadeta Killian analyses the performance of parliament in Tanzania in two consecutive periods: 1990-1995 and 1995-2000. She argues that the 1990-1995 parliament was guided by the intra-party mode, which created a set of compelling incentives for an intra-elite competition for policy influence emanating from the single party, Channa Cha Mapinduzi (CCM). The 1995-2000 parliament, on the other hand, was guided by the inter-party mode in which the behaviour of both MPs and ministers was largely influenced by their affiliation. She argues further that while the intra-party mode created a great opportunity for moving towards institutional autonomy and pluralism, the inter-party mode shifted the focus towards the preservation of power under pluralist competitive politics.

2

Methodology

Deogratias Rugaimukamu

Sample Survey Design
The development of sample surveys as the scientific technique for collection, analysis and interpretation of data has provided policy decision makers and planners with vital information on various basic facts essential for the formulation and execution of national development programmes. But to be useful, the sample survey has to be painstakingly designed. All the different stages involved in selecting the sample should be carefully considered and weighed against the precision of the information desired and the resources available.

The sample survey design appropriate for most large scale sample surveys is generally a *stratified multi-stage sample survey design*. The first step involved is to divide the whole area to be covered under the study into *strata*. Stratification is important because different geographical parts of the country (for example, districts) differ widely in their characteristics.

Sample design for the study of the role of members of parliament as representatives of the people

Coverage/survey population
The fieldwork was divided into two components. The first component aimed at involving ordinary citizens and the second at involving 150 constituency members of parliament. Whereas the fieldwork for the first component was carried out in a number of locations using university students as interviewers, the second component of the fieldwork was carried out in one place, Dodoma, during a parliamentary session, using senior academic staff as interviewers.

For the first component involving ordinary voters, the fieldwork was carried out in eight Research and Education for Democracy in Tanzania (REDET) pilot districts, which are:

Moshi Rural (rural)
Bukoba Rural (rural)
Mtwara Rural (rural)
Nzega (rural)
Zanzibar North "A" (rural)
Chake Chake (rural)
Arusha Municipality (urban)
Mbeya Municipality (urban)

For practical convenience, the research was carried out through the existing administrative structure of districts, wards, and villages.

Choice of clusters

Clusters, which are the ultimate units in the sample selection, are required to be compact clusters and to be unambiguously demarcated. Because of the well defined boundaries and the information available on administrative areas, these administrative areas qualified to be used as clusters. For this sample survey, villages being the smallest natural population groupings, were used for the rural areas because they are considered to be the best choice for clusters in this setting.

As regards the urban districts, where there are no villages, the preferred procedure would have been to use enumeration areas. However, since enumeration areas cannot be located without the appropriate maps, the selection of enumeration areas was omitted. In other words, this sampling stage was not carried out in the two municipalities of Arusha and Mbeya.

Sample size

The usual approach in selecting sample size is to consider the characteristic(s) to be estimated taking into consideration a researcher's pre-specified level of precision required for the particular estimate and of course, the cost of carrying out the research.

One of the most important practical aspects which should influence the choice of the sample size is the survey capability of the research organisation. A sample that is too large and exceeds the survey capability will result in poor organisation and control. Non-sampling errors might contribute significantly (in the absence of the consideration given) to the survey capability of the survey organisation. Also, the sample size will depend on the amount of desired domains of the survey. For this sample survey the desired domains were male/female and rural/urban.

In most research, the complicated step of analysing the cost function of the survey and the overall variance of the estimates in order to decide on sample sizes is usually avoided. Sometimes, a sample size is pre-specified basing on some known experience from within the same country or from outside it. From the available documentation, it would seem that the surveys that have been done in Tanzania have involved sample sizes of between 4 and 11 per cent of the population sizes.

Although it would have been more prudent to use a bit of the sampling theory to determine the sample size, it was considered acceptable to decide on the sample size based on what has been practised in Tanzania and elsewhere in the world. Accordingly, for this sample survey the choice of the sample size was largely determined by practical considerations. In the end, the chosen sample size was 640 households which meant 80 households for each of the 8 pilot districts.

Sampling design

Summary description of the survey design approach.

Voters' survey

The sample survey design for the voters' sample survey was a stratified five-stage sample design, starting with the wards, followed by the villages, the neighbourhood/street chairpersons, households, and individual respondents.

Selection of the wards/*shehia*

At the ward/*shehia* level, two wards or *shehia* were purposively selected based on the past REDET fieldwork of March and October 1997. In the March 1997, a survey of all the four wards was selected and in the October 1997, a survey of only one of the four wards was selected. Accordingly, for this survey two wards were purposively selected, one being the same as the October 1997 survey, while the other was randomly selected from the remaining three. This meant that fieldwork was carried out in only two of the 4 REDET wards/*shehia* of each pilot district. The locations in which fieldwork was carried out were as follows:

District	Wards/*Shehia*
Moshi Rural	Kibosho Magharibi and Mwika Kusini
Bukoba Rural	Maruku and Kyaka
Mtwara Rural	Ndumbwe and Mayanga
Nzega	Lusu and Mwangoye
Chake Chake	Wesha and Shungi
Zanzibar North "A"	Chaani Kubwa and Gamba

For the two municipalities of Arusha and Mbeya, two wards were selected randomly. The locations were as follows:

District	Wards
Arusha Municipality	Unga Limited and Ngarenaro
Mbeya Municipality	Luanda and Sisimba

Selection of the villages

From each of the selected wards/*shehia* the selection procedure would have been to choose two villages randomly. However, since the March 1997 and the October 1997 surveys were carried out in the same two villages of the wards, this time the fieldwork was carried out in the other two villages not covered in the earlier surveys with the exception of Chake Chake where all the villages were covered in the March and October 1997 surveys. Accordingly, the selected villages were as follows:

District	Ward	Villages
Moshi Rural	Kibosho Magharibi	Mkomongo, Kifuni
	Mwika Kusini	Mawanjeni, Kondeni
Bukoba Rural	Maruku	Maruku, Kyansozi
	Kyaka	Kyaka, Mushasha
Mtwara Rural	Ndumbwe	Ndumbwe, Mbuo
	Mayanga	Mkunwa, Kawawa

Nzega	Lusu	Ifumba, Mwasala
		Mwangoye
		Mwaguguli, Sagida

It should be noted that Zanzibar North "A" comprises *shehia* only and not villages.

For Chake Chake, this time, unlike during the March and October 1997 surveys when all villages were covered in the survey, two villages were randomly selected from each sampled *shehia*. The selection was as follows:

District	***Shehia***	**Villages**
Chake Chake	Wesha	Wesha, Mshangama
	Shungi	Chanjamjawiri, Michungwani

These villages were subsequently to be referred to according the voter's constituency demarcated for election purposes.

Selection of the neighbourhood/street chairpersons

For each of the two villages from the rural wards, three neighbourhood chairpersons were selected systematically from the list of neighbourhood/street chairpersons. That is a total of six chairpersons. The households under the first two chairpersons on the list for each village were then used for the sampling to get the required interviews and households under the third chairperson served as a reserve.

For each of the two urban wards, five street chairpersons were selected systematically from the list of street chairpersons. That is a total of ten chairpersons.

Again, the households under the first four chairpersons on the list were used in the sampling to get the required interviews and households under the fifth chairperson served as a reserve.

Selection of the households

In the case of rural wards, a list of the households under the jurisdiction of each of the two selected chairpersons was used. From the list of households of each chairperson, ten households were randomly selected. Thus, 20 households were picked from each village. In the case of urban areas and Zanzibar North "A" district, a list of the households under the jurisdiction of each of the four selected chairpersons was utilised. Then five households were randomly selected from the list of households of each chairperson. Thus, 40 households were selected from each ward.

The selection of a respondent in a household

For each sampled household only one person aged 18 years or above was to be interviewed. Furthermore, in any given household the interviewer knew before hand whether a man or a woman was to be interviewed.

In a household where a woman was to be interviewed, the interviewer listed all the women aged 18 or above. After the listing the interviewer selected randomly (using the provided table of random numbers) one of the listed women. The procedure was similar for the case where a man was to be selected from a household.

Members of parliament's survey

For the members of parliament's survey, a booklet called *Orodha ya Wabunge* (List of members of parliament) was used for sampling. The names in the book are listed under five categories: ministers, deputy ministers, shadow cabinet, parliamentary standing committee chairpersons, and other members. There were nine researchers and, accordingly, the first nine members of parliament were picked in each of the first four categories. Specifically, each researcher was assigned one minister, one deputy minister, one shadow cabinet member, and one parliamentary standing committee chairperson. As for other members of parliament, each researcher was assigned thirteen respondents. The circular method of allocation was used, that is starting with the first researcher, selected randomly, each researcher was allocated one member of parliament and then the process was repeated starting with the first researcher until each researcher was allocated twenty three respondents. Of the twenty three names, seventeen were for the required interviews and the remaining six were to serve as reserve for possible missed respondents.

Survey methodology and instruments

Every survey, no matter how simple, incurs costs. Furthermore, requirements for sample size and proper conduct of the fieldwork are demanding. The quality of the data obtained in a survey depends on the proper design of the questionnaire, on the sampling strategy and on good training and supervision of suitable interviewers.

Before the final decision to conduct a survey is made, three important questions should be answered: why are you doing the survey? how do you expect to use the results? and to whom and at what level the report results will be addressed to?

The answers to these questions should help to ensure that the survey will provide useful information for monitoring goals, for influencing policy and programme design and for encouraging policy makers and programme managers to allocate resources to social priority areas. What data is needed and how it may be used by policy makers, programme managers, communities and the general public.

Pilot survey

For any survey it is highly recommended to carry out at least one pilot study. The aim of the pilot survey is basically to test the adequacy of the survey instrument, assess the requirements for efficient supervision, and assess the enumeration processes covering all the participating parties, such as the headquarters, supervisors, and field enumerators. It is also used to record the likely extent of transportation problems in various areas. There was no pilot survey for the voters' survey simply because of the general feeling that the main problems were fairly known since the areas had been covered about three times before, although for different surveys. As it turned out, no unanticipated problems emerged.

Similarly, there was no pilot survey for the members of parliament survey, but in contrast with the voters' survey, this was later found to have been a very serious shortcoming. It was reported by the researchers that some parts of the questionnaire could have been modified to accommodate unanticipated responses which were eventually suggested by the interviewed members of parliament. Furthermore, the researchers noted in their reports that there are a number of important issues pertaining to the role and situation of members of parliament which the non-member of parliament could not possibly have anticipated and therefore were unwittingly and regrettably not captured by the questionnaire.

Training interviewers

It is essential to have high-quality data. This will be possible only if you allow enough time to train the supervisors and interviewers thoroughly. Before training starts, you should work out the field procedures to be followed during the survey. The primary document used for the training of interviewers for this survey was the fieldwork notes and the emphasis was on the careful handling of the questionnaire and the selection of the proper interviewees.

Questionnaire design

The questionnaire was the means for collecting information from the respondents.

In designing a questionnaire, it is necessary to be clear about its aims – to make sure the questionnaire for the survey is relevant to the specific purposes. It is advisable not to make the survey too long by including many unnecessary questions. It is always tempting to add more and more questions, expanding the survey unnecessarily. The temptation should be resisted and always the aim should be to collect only the minimum information needed for a particular study. Otherwise there will be a risk of overloading field workers, and demanding too much from respondents. Each question should have an explicit rationale for inclusion.

The main aim of a good survey instrument is to minimise the amount of error that can occur when measuring whatever it is you want to measure. This means that a good questionnaire can be used by interviewers to obtain answers that are both reliable and valid. By reliable, we mean that no matter who asks the question and no matter where and when it is asked, the same respondent would give the same answer. In a good questionnaire, the same question is asked in the same way by different interviewers – and differences between interviewers will be kept to a minimum. By valid, we mean that the question elicits a response that measures whatever it is you are interested in measuring and that the answer given to the question is true and accurate. A good questionnaire should enable you to obtain valid measures of the things you set out to measure, by helping to ensure that the respondent understands what information is being sought.

The other important aim of a good survey questionnaire is to obtain the necessary information quickly and easily. This means that as noted earlier, it should contain only the questions necessary to get the required information and both the interviewer and the respondents should easily understand these questions.

The contents of the questionnaire for this survey were developed by an expert and were discussed in two workshops called for that purpose. The final decision on the list of the topics was made by the REDET Programme Management Group. The questionnaire consisted of seven main sections:

- Personal particulars.
- Reasons for seeking to become a member of parliament.
- Adherence to representation principles and basis for representatives' actions.
- Relation of the representative with other political actors.
- Political competence of the member of parliament and the constituents/voters.
- Functions of the representative.
- Assessment of performance and reasons for success or failure.

Interview method

For the voters' questionnaire, the personal interview method was used and for each selected household in the sample, one person (female or male) aged 18 years and above was interviewed. The interviews were carried out in a structured way using a specifically designed questionnaire which was filled in by carefully and adequately trained interviewers. The training sessions covered such aspects as the nature, scope, and objectives of the investigation, how to respond to various problems that might arise, and how to behave during the survey. Furthermore, the interviewers were made to understand very well the implications of each and every question in the questionnaire.

Again, for the members of parliament questionnaire, the personal interview method was used but the arrangements were quite different. Although each researcher was originally allocated specific members of parliament to be interviewed, when the actual interviews started, some researchers found it necessary to interview any member of parliament who became available irrespective of the earlier agreed allocation. This was mainly because it was difficult to trace and interview members of parliament strictly by the allocated lists. As regards the recording of responses, there were both circling of pre-coded answers and writing of the exact wording of the respondent's reply by the interviewer.

Personnel

The number of interviewers for the survey very much depends on the resources available and of course, the period earmarked for fieldwork.

For the voters' survey, 16 second year Political Science students and eight senior academic staff were engaged as supervisors.

For the members of parliament's survey, nine senior academic staff were engaged as interviewers. Apart from these people, two other people were engaged for coding and data entry.

Survey documents and field operations

The main survey documents were the questionnaire, the interviewer's fieldwork notes, and a table of random numbers. After training, all the personnel dispersed to their work destinations. The field interviewers were equipped with introduction letters, questionnaires, and fieldwork notes. Each field enumerator was supposed to select the households to be visited for the interview. Replacement of missed sampled respondents was done according to research instructions.

Handling of the questionnaire

Each field supervisor was instructed to edit all questionnaires completed every day. At this time the supervisor was required to ensure that all the entries were correctly done and any doubts were cleared with the interviewer concerned. At the end of the fieldwork, the supervisor submitted the completed questionnaire together with a report on the field operations to the REDET Programme Administrator.

Substitution of households

If for some reason a selected respondent could not be interviewed at the first call, the interviewer was instructed to record that particular respondent for replacement. Interviewers were advised to continue recording the missed interviews as they went on interviewing in the households under selected chairpersons. After completing the interviewing in the households under selected chairpersons, sampling was subsequently made to obtain replacements of the missed interviews from the households on the reserve list.

The number of interviewees from the Mainland and Zanzibar

Although in the REDET 1994, baseline sample survey it was decided to over-sample Zanzibar, the over-sampling was much greater in this survey. Whereas 449 (9.6 per cent of the total) interviews were planned for Zanzibar during the REDET 1994 baseline sample survey, 160 (25 per cent of the total) interviews were planned for this survey. As a result, some of the characteristics may be overstated. Since religious affiliation differs greatly between the mainland and the islands, this over-sampling was bound to show a different pattern of religious affiliation from that recorded during the REDET 1994 baseline sample survey.

Publicity

Given the political background of Tanzania and its people, nothing, however trivial, which involves the people can be done successfully without informing and educating the masses. Thus, surveys of this kind have to be backed up by good publicity in order to achieve the best results. Accordingly, the REDET programme used its network of district facilitators, ward and village recorders to inform the people of the visits of the REDET survey researchers.

Data processing

After all the questionnaires had been received, the data was processed and analysed in accordance with the outline laid down for the purpose at the time of developing the research plan. Technically speaking, data processing implies editing, coding, presentation (which means classification, tabular and graphic presentation) of collected data so that they are amenable to the final stage of analysis. The term analysis refers to the computation of certain measures along with searching for patterns of relationships that exist among data groups.

Editing and coding

For this survey the main editing was done by the field supervisors before submitting the questionnaires. The final editing was the automatic cleaning of the data after or keying in the computer. As regards coding, the process had already been simplified by having a substantial number of pre-coded questions.

Data analysis

Data analysis mainly refers to computation of certain measures for either descriptive purposes or investigative ventures. One may investigate patterns of relationships between variables. Data analysis is highly dependent on the level of measurement of the data collected. Since the levels of measurement in the study were mainly nominal and ordinal, some of the statistical analysis which require interval and ratio measurement levels are not relevant. The Statistical Package and Software System (SPSS) was used to produce One-way and two-way frequency tables.

Problems faced during fieldwork

A number of problems emerged during the fieldwork. For the voters' survey the main problem was transport. A few sampled villages that were inaccessible by any means of transport were replaced by the supervisors in the field.

In contrast, the members of parliament survey faced many more problems than the voters' survey. First, it took more than a day to process the research clearance to interview members of parliament. Secondly, the timing of the survey was not very good. Members of parliament, particularly cabinet ministers were very busy winding up the parliamentary session, and therefore it was extremely difficult to carry out the interviews. Thirdly, identifying members of parliament selected for interviews was quite difficult. Since the researchers did not know most of the members of parliament personally, it took time to identify those selected for interviews. Fourthly, there were a number of broken promises and consequently, either time was wasted because members missed the interviews or turned up late by which time the researcher had arranged to interview somebody else.

Quality of the data

The quality of the data obtained highly depends on four things:
i) Sampling errors (a function of the sample size taken)
ii) Extent of complete non-response
iii) Extent of partial non-response
iv) Other non-sampling errors

Sampling and non-sampling errors

All types of investigations are vulnerable to errors in getting information on given aspects of a target population. Enquiries aimed largely at recording behavioural tendencies are probably in a slightly better position than those aimed at obtaining quantitative measurements. Nevertheless, in both cases there are often a number of formidable distortions or errors in information to contend with.

In choosing between complete enumeration (census) and sample survey, the two techniques available for data collection, researchers must always be aware of the identity.

Total error = sampling error + Non-sampling error.

The total error may in fact, turn out to be larger in complete enumeration than in a sample survey if the target population is very large. This is because in a well chosen small sample it is possible to engage superior (serious and dedicated) personnel, train and supervise them adequately at all the stages of the data collection process than would be in a complete enumeration. That is, the non-sampling errors tend to be larger in a census than in a sample survey when the area of investigation is very large.

Sampling errors

Sampling errors result from the design of the sample survey when the researcher decides to use the sample survey technique. Manifestly, since a sample is usually a small fraction of the target population, the sample must be well designed to minimise these sampling errors. Indeed, it is always advisable that the sample be selected in such a way as to allow for the estimation of the sampling errors to facilitate assessment of the generalisations of findings to the target population.

Unfortunately, as for all earlier REDET surveys, it has not been possible to compute the sampling errors. This is mainly because the lists (sampling frames) used at the different stages of sampling were not submitted together with the questionnaires, contrary to the given instructions. Also, since REDET surveys are multi-character in nature, appropriate prior computations need to be made, taking into consideration the extent of each character, if standard errors are to be calculated for each character. Furthermore, standard errors are vital when the research is aimed at obtaining estimates of certain attributes. Since the REDET surveys have so far, not aimed at obtaining estimates but have solely focused on capturing the general political orientation of the society, the standard errors are not so important. Indeed, the surveys done so far may still be regarded as tentative in nature.

All the same, it is imperative to get a feel of the data quality. One indirect procedure which at least points in the right direction, is to compare some of the sample characteristics with same characteristics displayed from other known surveys. An attempt is made here to compare a few aspects of the 1999 voters' survey to the characteristics obtained from the REDET 1994 baseline sample survey.

In Table 2.1 the percentage age distribution of the interviewees of the 1999 voters' survey is compared to that of the interviewees of the REDET 1994 baseline sample survey with respect to locality.

Methodology

Table 2.1: Age distribution recorded during the 1999 voter's survey and the REDET 1994 baseline sample survey in percentages

Age in years	1994 REDET baseline sample survey	1999 voter's sample survey
18 – 25	24.2	20.7
26 – 35	30.0	28.4
36 – 45	19.4	19.0
46 – 55	12.5	12.9
56 – 65	8.1	12.7
66 and above	5.8	6.3
Total	69.4	75.0

Source: Computations using REDET baseline and the 1999 voters' sample surveys findings.

As noted from Table 2.1, it may be said that although some differences are observed for a number of age groups, it is a bit reassuring that some percentages compare favourably for the two surveys.

In Table 2.2 the age distribution by sex from the 1999 voters' sample survey is compared to that from the REDET baseline sample survey.

Table 2.2: Age distribution: the 1999 voters' and the 1994 REDET baseline surveys by sex in percentages

Age in years	1994 REDET Baseline sample survey			1999 voters' sample survey		
	Female	Male	Total	Female	Male	Total
18 – 25	31.1	17.4	24.2	26.3	18.5	22.4
26 – 35	31.1	28.9	30.0	27.6	29.5	28.5
36 – 45	17.7	21.1	19.4	19.7	17.2	18.5
46 – 55	11.9	13.1	12.5	13.2	14.1	13.6
56 – 65	5.7	10.5	8.1	7.5	15.7	11.6
66 and above	2.4	9.0	5.8	5.6	5.0	5.3
Total	49.5	50.5	100	50.0	50.0	100

Source: Computations using 1999 voters' and REDET 1994 Baseline sample survey findings.

From Table 2.2, it seems that the female interviewees for age groups 18-25 and 26 –35 were slightly under-represented in the 1999 voters' survey compared to the 1994 baseline survey, but, in contrast, the female interviewees in the remaining age groups seem to be over-represented. As regards the male interviewees, it would seem that those in the 36 – 45 age group were under-represented in the 1999 voters' survey compared to the 1994 baseline survey, but those in age groups 56 – 65 and 66 and above were over-represented.

It should be noted, however, that this is just indicative because a conclusive interpretation can only be done on the basis of age distributions of the eight pilot districts covered. This is not necessary for the purposes of this exercise.

Generally speaking, the 1999 voters' sample survey findings seem fairly reassuring, since they tend to reasonably replicate the results obtained from the 1994 baseline sample survey.

In Table 2.3 below, the information on religion obtained during the REDET-II and the REDET baseline sample surveys is compared.

Table 2.3: Distribution of people according to religion: the 1999 voters' and the 1994 REDET baseline sample surveys, in percentages

Religious domenination	1994 baseline sample survey	1990 voters' sample survey
No religion	5.6	7.8
Traditional religion	0.9	0.2
Christian	62.8	42.9
Moslem	30.4	46.6
Other	0.1	1.6
Not stated	0.1	0.9
Total	100.0	100.0

Source: 1999 voters' and REDET 1994 baseline sample surveys findings.

It is noted from Table 2.3 that there are some appreciable differences in the figures on religious affiliation obtained from the two surveys.

However, as already alluded to earlier, these findings are not very surprising because of the greatly increased over-sampling of Zanzibar, which markedly affect the pattern of religious affiliation.

Apart from this observation, the 1999 voters' sample may be regarded as representative of the target population and therefore, would be expected to yield quality data if all the other operations are executed efficiently.

Non-sampling errors

Non-sampling errors affect the results of both sample surveys and complete enumeration though they tend to increase with the sample size. In many cases, non-sampling errors are much larger in complete enumeration than in well-conducted sample surveys.

Most sources of non-sampling errors concern field operations and data processing. During the planning of the REDET-II sample survey, steps were taken to lessen the effects of non-sampling errors by carefully looking at all the stages of the survey and discussing what could possibly go wrong. In the training of the field interviewers, all the things that needed to be avoided were pointed out in detail and discussed thoroughly. However, in spite of this careful training, there were some lapses when it came to the actual field work. During the data entry it was observed that a few interviewers were negligent and omitted recording responses to certain questions thus increasing the extent of partial non-response.

Extent of complete non-response

Of the 640 planned interviews, 639 were carried out, amounting to a 99.8 per cent coverage. Table 2.4 gives the planned and actual coverage by sex.

Table 2.4: 1999 voters' sample survey planned and actual coverage of female and male respondents

Area	Planned			Actual coverage		
	Female	Male	Total	Female	Male	Total
Mainland	240	240	480	240	239	479
Zanzibar	80	80	160	79	80	159
Tanzania	320	320	640	319	319	638

* Of the 639 respondents only one respondent's sex was not indicated.

Source: 1999 voters' sample survey.

Extent of partial non-response

Although there were a few instances where respondents refused to give responses to some questions, generally very good cooperation from the respondents was recorded.

References

Cochran, W G (1963). *Sampling Techniques.* Second edition. New York: Wiley International Edition.

Raj, Des, (1968). *Sampling Theory.* New Delhi: McGraw-Hill Publishing Company, Ltd.

REDET (1994). *Baseline survey data file.*

3

Historical and Theoretical Analysis of Representation

Samuel S. Mushi

Introduction

This chapter analyses representation as it has evolved historically in Western Europe and North America. We have two reasons for basing our analysis on the western liberal traditions. First, Tanzania and other Commonwealth countries are engaged in building western-type liberal democracies. Secondly, there is much more literature on the western-type representative government than on representational forms of other regions. The chapter is organised in six sections. Section 1 looks at representation in historical perspective. Section 2 examines the main principles of representation in liberal democracies. Section 3 explores the potential facilitators and constraints of representation. Section 4 discusses two representation models, namely the individualist model and the collectivist model. Section 5 sketches the main functions of the representative, and finally section 6 sums up the chapter.

Representation in historical perspective

The idea of democracy is believed to have originated in Greece. However, the great Greek political philosophers, namely Plato and Aristotle, knew nothing about representation and had no word for it. Neither the Greeks nor the Romans of antiquity built representative institutions. This was because face-to-face democracy was possible in the small city-states, and all male citizens could afford the time for direct participation in politics and governance because of the presence of the labour of the politically non-participant slaves and women (Friedrich, 1968).

Ideas of representation began to emerge from the political theories of the Middle Ages (fifth to fifteen century). These theories borrowed mainly from corporation law and the religious notion that the Head of the Catholic Church represented God on earth (Friedrich, 1968). The European medieval constitutional order had to include representative elements because, unlike the Greek city states, it applied to large territorial units in which direct participation by entitled citizens was impossible. The unitary organisation of the Catholic Church had necessitated the creation of representative assemblies in the form of councils. This practice was extended to the secular feudal order by giving corporate representation to cities, municipalities, towns and some rural shires in the emerging parliaments under monarchs. These monarch-controlled assemblies predated political parties and represented three classes (or estates as they were called), namely, the nobility, the clergy and the merchants (burgesses) of the cities. In the English Parliament of this period, the nobility and higher clergy sat in the House of Lords while burgesses sat in the House of Commons (Friedrich, 1968).

This representation was quite different from representation in the modern democratic state. First, representation was simply a political strategy of the king to get the powerful people (nobility, clergy and merchants) on his side and working for him. They reciprocated by helping the king to mobilise resources (taxes, etc.) from the community and themselves. Secondly, although the masses participated economically (as the main producers and tax payers), they did not participate politically and were, therefore, not represented in the institutions of governance. Thirdly, the representatives were accountable to the king who appointed them. At best, the representative defended his estate interests, for the notion of 'national interest' was still rudimentary.

The social contract political theorists of the seventeenth and eighteenth centuries took the idea of representation seriously, making it the pivot of their governance schemes and constructs. However, the three leading theorists – Thomas Hobbes, Jean Jacques Rousseau and John Locke - generated entirely different forms of representation. We shall look at these briefly. Thomas Hobbes' entire conception of the state rested upon the idea of representation. He stated:

'A multitude of men are made *one person* when they are by one man or one person represented for it is the unity of the representer not the unity of the represented, that make the person one ...unity cannot otherwise be understood in multitude.' (Friedrich,1968:272)

In other words, Hobbes argues that the only way to understand or achieve the unity of the state is in the context of all people agreeing (at some assumed point) on a covenant to make one person or an assembly of persons their representative and to be bound by the decisions and actions of the representative person or assembly. This avoids the chaos that would result from the multitude of people who differ greatly in their views and ambitions and who would search for 'power after power unto death.' This idea of super-imposition of one person over all others was consonant with the age of monarchical absolutism, but it has also given rise to totalitarian forms of representation in modern times, like the claim by communist parties to represent the proletariat. Such claims ignore the varied interests that exist in the community by emphasising unity through a representative who is not accountable to the community.

In his Social Contract, Rousseau, unlike Hobbes (his great antagonist) showed hostility to any kind of representation scheme. He argued that sovereignty cannot be represented and therefore, the deputies of the people are not its representatives, but merely its commissaries (i.e. delegates) who cannot make independent decisions. In keeping with his idea of the 'general will,' Rousseau argued that any law which has not been approved by the people is null and void. This anti-representation posture of Rousseau was partly influenced by the small self-governing cantons of his native Switzerland which provided a living model for active participation of the citizenry (Friedrich,1968).

In his writings on government and politics, Locke placed emphasis on such democratic values as personal freedoms and rights, government by consent of the people and the right of the people to call their government into accountability, including the right to revolt. The utilitarian philosophers of the nineteenth, century (especially John Stuart Mill) further elaborated on these values and added a new one, namely the view that the highest good lies in the greatest good of the greatest number. These liberal values ushered mass democracy in which representatives would be elected by and were accountable to the people in electoral constituencies. The sovereignty of the prince had given way to the sovereignty of the people.

The principles of representation in liberal democracies

We start with definitions of representation and representative government. Friedrich (1968:278) defines representation as follows:

> 'Representation is the process by and through which the political power and influence which the entire citizenry or a part of them might have upon governmental action is, with their express or implied approval, exercised on their behalf by a small number among them, with binding effect upon the whole community thus represented.'

Mill, (1963:104) defines representative government in much the same light:

> ' The meaning of representative government is that the whole people, or some numerous portion of them, exercise through deputies periodically elected by themselves the ultimate controlling power which, in every constitution, must reside somewhere. This ultimate power they must possess in all its completeness. They must be masters, whenever they please, of all the operations of government.'

From these definitions we can extract five essential principles of representation in a liberal democracy. These are that:

- The ultimate power lies with the people (the popular sovereignty principle);
- This popular power is exercised by a selected few on behalf of the many (the deputation principle);
- These deputies (or representatives) are mandated by the people through periodic elections (the popular consent principle);
- Decisions made and actions carried out by these deputies have a binding effect on the community (the governance principle); and
- As ultimate masters, the people remain the final judge of performance of the government and their deputies (the accountability principle).

These principles raise theoretical and practical problems. How should the representative act so as to conform to all the principles? The main debate has, historically, focused on whether the deputy or MP should be a delegate bound by an imperative mandate or one with a general, flexible mandate in which he can exercise discretion as a rational person. While Rousseau favoured a representative bound by a rigid mandate (as we have seen), Edmund Burke (an English philosopher and politician) argued for a representative with discretionary authority. He argued that the MP is not bound by a rigid mandate from his constituents. He is, rather, guided by four things, namely constituency opinions, rational judgement, consideration of the national interest and personal convictions or conscience. These four things came out clearly in his celebrated speech to his electors at Bristol in 1774; and we shall let his own words speak.[1]

Constituency views and opinions:

> 'To deliver an opinion is the right of all men; that of constituents is a weighty and respectable opinion, which a representative ought always to rejoice to hear; and which he ought always most seriously to consider.'

Rational judgement

> 'My worthy colleague (i.e. his opponent for the Bristol seat) says his will ought to be subservient to yours. If that be all, the thing is innocent. If government were a matter of will upon any side, yours, without question, ought to be superior. But government and legislation are matters of reason and judgement, and not of inclination; and what sort of reason is that, in which the determination precedes the discussion; in which one set of men deliberate, and another decide..?'

> '...authoritative instructions, mandates issued, which the member is bound blindly and explicitly to obey, to vote and to argue for, though contrary to the clearest conviction of his judgement and conscience; these are things utterly unknown to the laws of this

---

[1] The speech is to be found in Edmund Burke, Writings and Speeches, Vol. II (Boston, 1901), pp. 89-98. Our order of quoting does not follow the order of the speech.

land and which arise from a fundamental mistake of the whole order and tenor of our constitution.'

National interest:

'Parliament is not a congress of ambassadors from different and hostile interests; which interests each must maintain, as an agent and advocate, against other agents and advocates; but parliament is a deliberative assembly of *one nation* with *one intere*st, that of the whole; where not local purposes, not local prejudices ought to guide, but the general good.'

Representative convictions and conscience:

'His (i.e. representative's) unbiased opinion, his mature judgement, his enlightened conscience, he...does not derive from your (i.e. constituents') pleasure; no, nor from the law and constitution... they are a trust from providence, for the abuse of which he is deeply answerable.'

A functional analysis of these views would yield three functions of the Burkean ideal representative, namely functions based on the views, opinions and interests of the constituents; functions or activities originating from the representative's own judgement of the situation as well as personal convictions and conscience, and functions or decisions based on consideration of the national interest. We shall return to the question of functions of the representative in section five. Suffice it to conclude here that most people now tend to view a representative in Burkean terms: a person with discretion and inclined or expected to act in response to local, national and personal exigencies.

Potential facilitating and constraining factors of representation

Structural, cultural and economic factors may affect the efficacy of representation positively or negatively. We shall review these factors briefly.

Political structure variables

There are many structural variables which affect the performance of a representative. We can only mention the more significant ones here, indicating briefly how they might affect the work of the representative.

Party system: One-party v. multiparty system. In general, representatives tend to be more party-controlled under the one-party system. Lacking independent platform, they have limited 'political space' in which to distinguish themselves. Non-conformity with the party line often amounts to a ticket to the political wilderness.

Political system: parliamentary v. presidential system, and unitary v. federal system. If we restrict out comparison to the British and American systems, the representative is more constrained by the assembly-cabinet fusion, the stronger party whip and emphasis on 'party government' in the British parliamentary, unitary system than in the American presidential, federal system where branches of government are separated, power is decentralised and parties have weaker assertions and control over representatives (see section four for elaboration).

Electoral system: single-member constituency, first-past-the-post (or winner-take-all) v. proportional representation. Among other things, the former facilitates closer representative-constituency relations, while the latter induces the representative's loyalty to his party rather than to a population in a unit area. In short, electoral systems can determine the "representativeness" of the representative.

Parliament types: unicameral v. bicameral type. In general, other things being equal, representatives in a unicameral parliament can act faster and are better placed to exercise control over the other branches than representatives in a bicameral parliament. As Wall, (1987:417) observes, the framers of the US constitution adopted the bicameral parliamentary system so as to limit the possibility of the Congress dominating the presidency and the Supreme Court. The bicameral structure 'not only secured representation of different interests but also limited the power of the legislature which, when hobbled by two houses often working against each other, could not act as swiftly and forcefully as a single body could.'

Power distribution among the three branches of government: balanced v. unbalanced distribution. Unbalanced distribution disables the representative (and the representative body) to perform one of the essential functions, namely to countercheck (or control) actions of the Executive and its elaborate bureaucracy. If representatives cannot control the executive which controls the resources, they may as well be tamed by the Executive's bureaucratic agencies so as to ensure that resources trickle down to their constituencies. A presidential power of dissolution, for instance, impairs an MP's effectiveness as a spokesperson of the people. For example, in 1973 President Nyerere of Tanzania forced refractory MPs to pass an unpopular income tax bill by simply threatening to dissolve Parliament. MPs are particularly susceptible to such threats where Parliament has no power to retaliate (e.g. the 'no confidence' motion).

Power distribution in society: unitary v. federal systems, and central v. local government. In general, decentralised systems (whether in unitary or federal structures) afford the representative more resources and leverage for independent action in the local communities than centralised systems. This facilitates the constituency servicing function of the representative.

State of the civil society: articulate v. latent interests. The amount and quality of work the representative does in his constituency is in part a function of the push from the 'articulate' interests in the constituency. Furthermore, a strong public opinion on public issues helps the representative to perform the function of shaping public policy or to extract resources from central and local government agencies to meet constituency needs. James Madison, the fourth President of the US, 1809-17 who helped to draft the US Constitution and Bill of Rights, stated: 'It is a sound and important principle that the representative ought to be acquainted with the interests and circumstances of his constituents – to which the authority and care of the representative relates' (Woll, 1987:420). Again, as Dye and Ziegler (1981) suggest, 'Representatives have to work with politically relevant elites in the constituency if they are to be effective: A congressional member's relevant political constituency is not the general population of the district but the elite of the district. We should think of a constituency not as an aggregate body of people but as relatively small group of political activists. Such activists are those with time, interest, and skill to communicate about political events. Consequently, they are of disproportionately high social status, (sometimes) as high as (or higher than) their representatives.'

Political culture variables

Almond and Verba (1963) have given us both a methodology and a set of concepts which can be used in studying and discussing the subject of political culture. REDET's own work on Tanzanian political culture has thrown much useful light on the orientations of various segments of the population towards politics in general and public authorities in particular (Mushi *et al*, 1998). Here we shall mention only the variables which we think can have significant effect on the work of the representative.

Political competence of the citizenry: Political competence of the citizens is affected by, among other things, the following: established historical traditions; norms and beliefs; levels of education; literacy and political awareness; established channels of information flow and the habit of the people to acquire information. The hypothesis is that a politically competent citizenry is more likely to produce industrious representatives than an incompetent citizenry. In other words, a society gets a representative it deserves.

MP's perception of his/her role and power: Generally, people will do what they are *expected* to do and will use the power which they *believe* they have. The MP's perception of his 'political space' will affect what he does. How does he assess his power and authority in the constituency and nationally? How does he view his relations with his party and the government locally (within the constituency) and nationally? Does he have a personal identity, e.g, personal manifesto or programme – or does he see himself just as a person who implements his party's manifesto and programme? Representatives will differ on role and power perception variables partly depending on the political culture obtaining in the country or culture to which they have been subjected in the past.

Expectations of constituents: What do constituents understand to be the role of an MP? Do they make a distinction between the constituency-level and national-level role of the representative? Research in the United States has shown that voters do make a distinction between the congressman as an individual representative and Congress as an institution. While the individual congressman is judged for his personality, style and constituency work, the Congress, as an institution, is judged by its ability to recognise and solve the nation's problems.

Economic variables

Generally, representation effectiveness varies with the economic power of the country. Representation functions require a lot of resources and willingness by the government to allocate them for that purpose. Examples of the leading resource consuming areas include: attractive compensation to be able to get and retain talented people in representation work; transport to enable the representative to make wide contacts in his constituency; and research funds to enable the representative to acquire adequate information regarding the activities of various government departments and agencies. Without such information he cannot be effective in the governance realm.

Representation models: Individuals and collectivist

Our discussion so far would suggest two contrasting models of representation. These can be called *individualist* and *collectivist* models. We shall present their main features briefly.

The individualist model

The individualist model promotes to the maximum the freedom and efforts of the individual politician or representative. This model originated from European and American liberalism of the eighteenth and nineteenth centuries. Samuel Beer (1974:84) provides a good description of how the model operated in Britain during the nineteenth century:

> 'The liberal period in Britain produced versions of popular government that would be hard to reconcile with party government as it is known in Britain in recent times.. Nineteenth-century Liberals and Radicals were highly individualistic in their approach to politics as well as economics. In their view, the basic unit of representation was not a class or community, but the individual, rational man.'

> 'The importance of 'conscience' was much in the minds of these offspring of liberalism and religious dissent. On their premises party

discipline and strong party organisation could not easily be justified. The highest respect was reserved for the independent politician, not in the sense of one who was outside the party but of one who was in the party solely because of conscientious opinion.'

'So while parties did develop in this period and party organisation began slowly to be built up throughout the country, in the legislature cross-voting was common and party cohesion very low. The middle period of the nineteenth century was, in the words of one historian, the golden age of the independent M.P.'

Framers of the US constitution deliberately established structures for maximising individual freedom and a culture of political and economic individualism has been created over the years. Although the rise of mass democracy since the second half of the nineteenth century necessitated the organisation of politics around political parties rather than around individual politicians, the US was able to preserve a larger 'political space' for the representative than in most European countries. The historical anti-party sentiments in the US has helped to limit the extent of 'bureaucratisation of politics' within the party, thus leaving relatively wide space for the representative's independent actions. For example, the representatives can and often do, individually or collectively, use congressional 'power of the purse' to ensure that government departments and agencies extend needed services to their constituencies. They lobby these agencies (which are themselves involved in lobbying the representatives for programme financing) directly without involving the parties. Thus, today the US remains the best example of the individualist representation model. We shall, therefore, discuss the main features of this model in the context of the United States, focusing on the following ten structure and culture variables:

- Extent of decentralisation of authority and resources
- Political orientation and freedom of civil society organisations
- Party control over representatives
- Government control over representatives
- Voters' control over representatives
- Party solidarity/cohesion
- Partisanship

- Representative's loyalty and accountability
- Election manifestos
- Organisation of campaigns

We have room for only sketchy notes on these variables.

Extent of decentralisation: there is substantial decentralisation of authority and resources due to federalism, but without weakening central institutions. This enables the representative to mobilise resources for his constituency both locally and nationally.

Freedom of civil organisations: US civil organisations, which number in their thousands, have clear independence from the government and political parties. They aggregate and articulate interests through sophisticated lobbying methods, the government and the legislature being the main targets. Individual Congressmen find these organisations handy in promoting the welfare of their constituencies and in cultivating support for the next election. 'Independent' representatives and independent civil organisations tend to be good allies in the political arena.

Party control over representatives: There is relatively weak party control over actions of their representatives. Although each Congressman seeks support of the local party organisation, he remains free to make use of other organisations which may not necessarily be affiliated to his party.

Government control over representatives: There is balanced power relations due to the doctrine of separation of powers. Independence of each 'power' from the others is emphasised by the separate presidential and congressional elections. It is true that the government controls most of the resources which the representative needs to service his constituency, but the representative has to authorise the budget, has to approve key appointments, and has the impeachment power. Thus the control that exists is mutual, based on reciprocity.

Voters' control over representatives: There is strong voter control due to frequent elections. Members of the House of Representatives are elected every second year; and a third of the Senators is also elected every second year. This encourages representatives who want to be re-elected to be in constant touch with and do good work for their constituencies.

Party solidarity/cohesion: There is relatively weak party solidarity or cohesion compared to European – especially British parties. US parties find it difficult to 'whip into line' their members and their representatives, for there is relatively strong accent on personal conscience. Beer (1974:84) attributes this low party cohesion to non-adherence to the doctrine of 'party government': 'In the United States the doctrine of party government has never taken deep hold in either the opinions or behaviour of people in practical politics. Here the older doctrine of political individualism still prevails.'

Partisanship: There is low partisanship in the US for the same reasons that there is low party solidarity. Most 'members' of a party are not card-carrying members as is the case in Britain and other parts of the world. People are members of particular parties by family tradition. This situation makes it possible for personality factors to take precedence over partisan considerations in elections.

Representative's loyalty and accountability: The representative's primary loyalty and accountability is to the voters and secondly to his party. This is because, as we have seen, the voters have relatively strong hold on their representatives due to frequent elections.

Election manifestos: In the US system, there is room for party as well as personal manifestos, with party manifestos outlining broad policies and actions and personal manifestos detailing the constituency level actions which the candidate/representative intends to undertake so as to meet perceived needs of his constituents. Parties do not try to pre-empt their candidates or force them to just harp on the party manifesto.

Organisation of campaigns: Although the local, constituency level party organisation plays an important role in organising campaigns for their candidates, there is plenty of room for personal election machines (e.g, committees). These personal machines play a role as great as, sometimes greater than, that of the local party organisation.

The collectivist model

The collectivist model began to emerge from the latter part of the nineteenth century. Proponents tried to show that political individualism had proved wanting for two main reasons. First, struggles of the working people had transformed politics from elite to mass democracy. During the elite politics era, voters in most European countries did not exceed five – ten per cent of the population due to limited franchise. This proportion rose gradually to reach over 50 per cent of the population in the course of the twentieth century. The rise of mass politics had necessitated transformation of class-based parties into well-organised, disciplined mass parties so as to cope with the task of mass mobilisation and membership recruitment on a national scale. This in turn necessitated the shift from individual-based to party-based politics and government. Thus emphasis was to be on the party and 'party government' (what we earlier referred to as the bureaucratisation of politics) rather than on the individual politician or representative.

The second argument was that local, constituency interests should be subordinate to national interests which can best be championed by the party rather than individual MPs. Edmund Burke put up such an argument in 1770 in his *Thoughts on the Present Discontent*. He said a 'party is a body of men united for promoting by their joint endeavours the national interest, upon some particular principle in which they are all agreed' (Beer, 1974:84) This Burkean view of a political party is based on a conception of the 'common good' which can only be achieved by a body of men and women working in concert over a long period of time.

Today, British politics provide the best example of the collectivist representation model. We shall, therefore, discuss the main features of this model in the context of the present British set up, and we shall use the same ten variables to provide contrast with the US individualist model.

Extent of decentralisation: There is relatively limited decentralisation of authority and resources due to unitarism.

Independence of civil organisations: They tend to be partisan and aggregate and articulate interests through political parties or lobby bureaucrats directly. Their relations with MPs are through party machinery.

Party control over representatives: There is a very strong party whip which requires representatives to stick to the party line. This limits the independence of representatives.

Government control over representatives: There is relatively strong government control over representatives due to the assembly-cabinet fusion in the parliamentary system, the emphasis on 'party government' (whose prime minister can dissolve parliament) and the strong party whip. The whip weakens the retaliatory weapons the representatives have, namely the 'power of the purse' and the 'motion of no confidence.'

Voters' control over representatives: Control of the voters over their representatives is relatively weak because the MP has a long tenure of five years and there are no 'recall' provisions.

Party solidarity/cohesion: Party solidarity or cohesion receives primary emphasis and is the most distinguishing feature of the collectivist model. In contrast to the individualist model, the political culture of the collectivist period attributes to the party quite a different function and a far higher claim to solidarity. Independent voting in the name of conscience is seen with a much more critical eye. Party solidarity and the pre-eminence of 'party government' receive priority over the efforts of the individual MP in Britain and most of the Commonwealth countries. Clement Attlee, the former British Labour prime minister, once ridiculed MPs who sought independence to vote according to their conscience. He said:

> 'In my experience, a good deal of so-called independence owes more to a desire for notoriety than to conscience. There are some people who delight in 'holier than thou' attitude. I recall an old Labour MP, Tom Shaw, saying to me, 'When I was young I was always talking about my conscience, but one day I realised that what I called conscience was my own blooming conceit. (Beattie 1970:550)'

There is an interesting example which illustrates the big difference between the US individualist and the British collectivist approaches to the party solidarity variable. In 1970 a British Labour Minister (R.H.S. Crossman) gave a lecture to an American audience explaining the meaning of the party mandate and how it 'bound' Labour MPs to vote together. A disgusted US legislator in the audience expressed his doubts about 'the morality of the member of parliament voting in a way other than how he believes.' Then the Labour Minister responded:

> 'There is no difficulty here because the MP is a member of the party and the MP is bound, therefore, by conference decision... If

he doesn't like that, he is not in the party and as for the morality, of course, his duty as a party member is to accept the constitution of the party. I can't understand what you're saying. (Beer,1974:85)'

The MP has relatively little room for independent action because of the great emphasis on party solidarity and party/ government line.

Partisanship: There is relatively strong partisanship because, first, the British are very class-conscious and secondly, party solidarity is a value which receives systematic emphasis. People become members by paying prescribed fees and carrying party cards.

Representative's loyalty and accountability: Going by the principle of popular sovereignty, primary loyalty should go to the electors. In practice, however, this principle is compromised under the collectivist model. Loyalty and accountability of representatives are shared among the voters, the party and the party government. In fact, it is the party rather than the voters who can call the MPs into accountability during inter-election periods, for, as we have seen, the British voters give their representatives a long tenure of five years, and cannot recall them before the next election. As for the MP himself, he cannot even give primary accountability and loyalty to his own conscience.

Election manifestos: The emphasis on solidarity leaves little room for personal manifestos because the party candidate has to stick to the party programme or be axed.

Organisation of campaigns: Constituency-level party organisation plays a more prominent role in organising the campaign for its candidate than personal election machines.

The features of the two models are given in summary form in Table 3.1 for ease of comparison.

Table 3.1 The leading features of the US individualist and the British collectivist representation models

	Structural and cultural variables	Orientation, tendencies and inclinations	
		The individualist model (US)	The collectivist model (UK)
1.	Extent of decentralisation of authority and resource	Substantial due to federalism	Relatively limited due to unitarism
2.	Political orientation of civil society organisations	Largely independent of party and government, aggregate and articulate interests through lobbying government and legislature	They tend to be partisan, and lobby party and government primarily and the legislature secondarily.
3.	Party control over representatives	Weak party whip	Strong party whip
4.	Government control over representatives	Balanced power relations due to separation of powers	Relatively strong control due to assembly cabinet fusion and emphasis on 'party government'
5.	Voter's control over representatives	Strong due to frequent elections	Weak due to five yearly elections without 'recall' provisions
6.	Party solidarity/cohesion	Weak	Strong
7.	Partisanship	Weak	Strong
8.	Representative's loyalty and accountability	Primarily to voters and secondarily to one's party	Loyalty/acountability divided among voters, one's party and party government
9.	Election manifesto	There is equal room for party and personal manifesto	Eminence given to party manifesto only
10.	Organising of campaign	Independent personal election machines play a role as great as and sometimes greater than that of the local party or organisation	Eminence given to party machines: personal actions usually coordinated within local party organisation

Functions of the representatives

Apart from the usual functions given in the constitution such as law-making, revenue raising, authorisation of budgets, etc., members of parliament do a lot other things sanctioned by convention, expectations of the voters, personal convictions and the fact that they are 'leaders.' It is, therefore, not possible to list all the activities that an MP *may* do because much depends on his personal initiative and the push from constituents. However, we have sieved what we believe to be the leading functions against which performance can be assessed. These functions are conceived at three levels – national, constituency and personal.

National level functions include law-making; passing and amending the constitution; approving taxes, other revenues and budgets; making or shaping public policy; controlling government actions; informing the government about constituency situations; resource allocation nationally and providing leadership nationally.

Constituency level functions include informing his or her constituency about government actions, plans and policies; helping to settle conflicts and resolve grievances of constituents; aggregating and articulating interests of constituents to relevant authorities; resource allocation locally; mobilising efforts for the development of the constituency; providing leadership locally.

Personal level functions include self-advertising, credit claiming and position taking.

The national-level and constituency-level functions listed above are well known and require no elaboration here. The personal-level functions are less known and we shall discuss them briefly.

Self-advertising has been defined by Mayhew (1987:469) as 'any effort to disseminate one's name among constituents in such a fashion as to create a favourable image but in message having little or no issue content.' Getting oneself known in the constituency and nationally requires a lot of self-advertising work. Mayhew estimates that in the United States only about half the electorate, if asked, can supply their House members' names. Methods of getting known include the following:
– frequent visits to the constituency
– speeches to home audiences

- attending constituents' functions and ceremonies, such as weddings and burials
- sending letters of condolences or congratulations to constituents
- writing newspaper columns
- participating in public debates (on radio and TV, in seminars, conferences, etc.)
- being calculatingly vocal on selected issues of local and/or national importance.

Credit claiming has been defined as 'acting so to generate a belief in a relevant political actor (or actors) that one is personally responsible for causing the government, or some unit thereof to do something that the actor (or actors) considers desirable. ...The emphasis here is on individual accomplishment (rather than, say, party or government accomplishment) and on the Congressman as doer (rather than as, say, expounder of constituency views)' (Mayhew, 1987:469)

Position taking is defined as 'the public enunciation of judgemental statement on anything likely to be of interest to political actors.' The position taken may tie with constituency interests, or party position on the issue, or personal conscience. The position may be conservative (i.e. clinging to one's position of the past), or radical (i.e. breaking with the past or the mainstream view). Position taking includes fence-sitting on some sensitive issues if the representative is uncertain of the consequences of his pronouncement – i.e. how his constituents or his party would receive it.

These three personal-level functions should not be considered selfish actions and the representative should not be accused of 'blowing his trumpet.' For he cannot be known unless he advertises himself, he cannot get credit unless he claims it and he cannot distinguish himself unless he takes a position on issues which are considered important locally or nationally. These functions are important for two main reasons. First, they determine whether the representative will make it or flop politically. No MP can get the honour of being considered a great parliamentarian or a first rate constituency representative unless he performs these personal-level functions well. Secondly, success in these functions may also induce success at the constituency level and national level functions listed above. Thus, although the three levels compete with each other for the MP's time and other resources, they also reinforce each other if the MP is able to maintain a good balance among them.

It should be obvious by now that the two representation models treat these personal-level functions quite differently. While the individualist model promotes them, the collectivist model constrains them. In the collectivist model, the party and party government are glorified, the representative's earned credit is shared with the party and the government and the position he takes on major issues will have to be consistent with the party line.

Conclusion

The research findings in this volume on the role of the MPs as representatives of the people was guided by the historical and theoretical issues raised in this chapter. Thus, the survey instrument focused on the following five issues: (1) the extent of adherence to the five representation principles; (2) the extent to which the four bases of representative's actions (constituency views and opinions; rational judgement; national interest and representative's convictions and conscience) are honoured by MPs; (3) the relationship of the MPs with other political actors; (4) the political competence of the constituents (voters) and their MPs, and (5) the perceived as well as the actual role played by the MPs.

It is expected that the study will tell us something about the nature of Tanzania's democratic transition. Is it just emulating the liberal model or charting out a path of its own?

References

Almond, G, and Verba, S. (1963). *The Civic Culture: Political Attitudes and Democracy for Five Nations*, New Jersey: Princeton University Press.

Beattie, A. (1970). *English Party Politics*, Vol. II. London.

Beer, S.H. (1974). *The British Political System*, New York: Random House Inc.

Dye, T.R., and Zeiglar, L.H. (1981). *The Irony of Democracy*, California: Duxbury Press

Friedrich, C.J. (1968). *Constitutional Government and Democracy: Theory and Practice in Europe and America* (4th Ed), Massachusetts: Blasdell Publishing Company.

Mayhew, D. (1987) 'Congress: the election connection' in Woll, P. *American Government: Readings and Cases.*

Mill, J.S. (1963), 'Of the Proper Functions of Representative Bodies' In H. Eckstein and D. Apter, (eds). *Comparative Politics: A Reader.* New York: The Free Press.

Mushi, S.S. Mukandala, R. and Baregu, M. (eds). (1998). *Tanzania's Political Culture: A Baseline Survey,* Dar es Salaam: Department of Political Science and Public Administration.

Woll, P. (1987). *American Government: Readings and Cases.* (9th ed), Boston: Little, Brown and Company.

4

The ups and downs of the Tanzanian Parliament 1961-1994

Kapwepwe I. Tambila

Introduction

Lessons from the pre-independence period
At independence in 1961, Tanganyika was bequeathed a Westminster model parliament through the 'Tanganyika Order in Council,' a law passed in London earlier that year. However, Tanganyika had not been prepared legally and in practice to operate a liberal democratic parliamentary system. Colonialism in Tanganyika, as elsewhere in the world, had not been a school in democratic practice. On the contrary, it was a school in despotism and paternalism – it was a school in arrogant racism.

From 1890, when the German Imperial Government took over control in German East Africa from chartered company rule, to 1961 when independence was granted, Tanganyika was under absolute rule of governors representing the German and British governments.

On 1 October 1926 Sir Donald Cameron, the British Governor of Tanganyika, established the 'Tanganyika (Legislative Council) Order in Council, 1926' a Legislative Council (LEGCO), the precursor of parliament. Mwakyembe (1985) has described this council as an extension of the governor's office. It was only a preserve of European and Asian officials or non-official appointees of the Governor. Africans were represented in a very paternalistic fashion by a European who was supposed to take care of their interests. They themselves were relegated to so-called tribal authorities by a system of governance called indirect rule started the same year.

On 24 November, 1945, two African chiefs were appointed to the LEGCO. By 1948, there were four Africans, three of whom were chiefs and one a school teacher (Mwakyembe, 1985). The 'extension of the governor's office' continued up to 1958, when a new law brought slight changes. This ordinance, which came into force in 1958, broadened the franchise and changed the composition of the LEGCO. There was a limited African franchise: Eligible African voters were supposed to have eight years of education, be 21 years of age, have an annual income of three thousand shillings, be literate in either English or Kiswahili or be an office holder in government.

The composition of the LEGCO consisted of (a) the speaker, (b) ex-officio members to number up to seven, (c) nominated (appointed) members not to exceed the figure 34, including the ex-officio members, (d) 30 elected representatives consisting of ten Europeans, ten Asians and ten Africans, (e) up to three representatives appointed by the Governor to represent special interests and finally (f) temporary members.

It is obvious that elected members of the Council were out numbered by ex-officio and appointed members. Therefore, up to 1960, the only live lesson the people of Tanganyika – young and old alike – had obtained in running a 'democratic' government system was one of an undemocratic, racial, paternalistic and unrepresentative Legislative Council.

In 1960, the government instituted a committee led by Richard Ramage to look anew into possibilities of extending the franchise. The committee recommended the abolition of representation by race. It sought to extend the franchise by recommending that the qualifications be one of the following three: (i) ability to read and write in English or Kiswahili; (ii) having an annual income of 1,500 shillings, or (iii) being in the service of the government (Mwakyembe, 1985)

Therefore, the 'Responsible Government' LEGCO, which was constituted in 1960 after elections on 30 August, 1960, had a majority of elected members. Out of eighty-one members, seventy-one were elected and only ten were appointed. Considerations of race were still being effected. In 1960, of the seventy-one elected representatives, ten seats were reserved for Europeans and 11 were reserved for Asians (Mwakyembe, 1985). Therefore, if there was any period of learning to run a Westminster model liberal democratic parliamentary system before independence, the period was between September 1960 and December 1961, a very short period of only *15 months*!

The ups and downs of parliament

The concept of parliamentary sovereignty
The ups and downs of parliament can be measured by looking at the power structure between the three arms of the state namely, the legislature, the executive and the judiciary. The executive includes all institutions of government and the process *of electing the president*. It is 'supported by the twin pillars of the bureaucracy and the party' (MacAuslan and Ghai, 1972:196-7). The legislature and the judiciary are institutions of control which, each in its own way and limited by its constitutional competence, exercise control over the executive and other institutions of government.

Other important institutions of control are the system of elections to the National Assembly and the Permanent Commission of Inquiry. The members of the National Assembly are elected by the electorate who are the ultimate supreme. It has been claimed that through source of power and sovereignty the electoral system 'the government is made aware of people's views and feelings, more important, perhaps, the people themselves become aware of their own ultimate sovereignty, as candidates are removed and replaced by fresh talent,' (MacAuslan and Ghai, 1972:202).

This control is put into effect through political parties, acting both locally and centrally. At the local level, the parties nominate candidates whom are expected, if elected, to represent local interests and articulate local problems to the government at the centre. The implications of the system of nomination at central level in so far as it impinges on the freedom of the legislature itself and therefore the exercise of its sovereignty, which is an expression of the sovereignty of the people, will be commented upon later.

The ultimate objective of elections is to bring into being an assembly that will act as an institution of control. Control here means political control i.e. 'the possibility of influencing those who hold power in such a way that they take into account the interests of those exerting the control' (MacAuslan and Ghai, 1972). The effectiveness of the National Assembly as an institution of control can be determined therefore from the very process of its formation, its composition, functions and operations.

The independence constitution : A Westminster model parliament

Elements of a Westminster model parliament include: (i) the existence of many competing political parties; (ii) the practice of one person one vote during elections; (iii) the practice of liberal democracy; (iv) parliament being the central institution of government; (v) parliament being sovereign; (vi) practice and procedures in parliament follow those of the British one, also known as 'the Mother of Parliament;'(vii) a Governor-General represents the king/queen as ceremonial head of state; (viii) the prime minister being the wielder of real power; (ix) the existence of a prime ministerial and cabinet system; (x) the existence of a loyal opposition; (xi) the existence of an independent and impartial judiciary and finally (xii) the existence of an impartial civil service and armed forces (Mwakyembe,1985).

The most important element of the independence constitution was *that parliament was supreme.* It exercised direct control over legislation. Parliament was omnipotent and omnicompetent in respect of legislation. It had overall authority over the cabinet because the National Assembly could remove the entire cabinet from office by passing a motion of no confidence in the government.

In such an event the prime minister was supposed to resign or to advise the governor-general to dissolve parliament. If the prime minister did not resign within three days or 72 hours, the governor-general was bound to dissolve parliament. He could also remove the prime minister without dissolving parliament if the resolution was passed within 14 days after a general election and the governor-general found it possible to replace the prime minister without dissolving parliament.

Parliamentary supremacy went in tandem with the core element of government responsibility under the system: *The prime minister and his cabinet were collectively responsible to parliament for any advice given to the governor-general and for all things done by or under the authority of any minister in the execution of his office* (Mwaikusa,

1995). Responsibility was to parliament and not to the governor-general.

If the prime minister was removed or changed, ministers lost their offices automatically. This was the doctrine of collective ministerial responsibility, which was stated expressly in the constitution.

The constitution also ensured that the judiciary was impartial and independent. The chief justice was appointed by the governor-general on the advice of the prime minister. The other judges were appointed by the governor-general on the advice of the Judicial Service Commission and not on the advice of the prime minister. High Court judges had security of tenure meaning that once appointed, the appointing authority, namely the governor-general could not remove them. Their removal had to go through other very specific procedures (Mwaikusa, 1995). Other officers of the judiciary were appointed, disciplined and/or removed from office by the Judicial Service Commission. These arrangements were made in order to make sure that the judiciary was independent of the executive.

Two other officers were treated like judges. These were the incumbents of the offices of the Auditor-General and the Director of Public Persecutions (DPP). They were free from control by the executive arm of government and had security of tenure. Their remuneration came directly from the Consolidated Fund. Like parliament and the judiciary, these offices were responsible for supervising the executive and had thus to be independent of the executive.

At independence, parliament started without a 'loyal opposition' envisaged by the Westminster model. The Tanganyika African National Union (TANU) won by a massive landslide. They took 71 out of the 71 seat National Assembly. Even the seat won by Mr Herman Sarwatt as an independent, was, in a way, a TANU seat because Sarwatt was an active TANU member (Mwakyembe, 1985).

The independence constitution allowed members of parliament a lot of freedom to criticise the government on many issues, continuing the tradition begun in the pre-independence Legislative Council. In the LEGCO, for example, radical members pressed for the 'Africanisation' of the civil service, criticised the government for being too moderate and slow in implementing its policy of abolishing race-based separate schools and bitterly complained about and strongly objected to the granting of automatic citizenship to non-African residents born in Tanganyika and had at least one of their parents born in the country (Mwaikusa, 1995).

After independence, one of the hottest debates concerned the issue of Tanganyika becoming a republic within the Commonwealth of Nations. Members of parliament spoke freely, challenged the government and elicited answers, which were weighed. Indeed, observers of the early independence years' political scene have noted that both the ruling party and the executive acknowledged the *supremacy* of parliament in spirit and in action as the 'constitutionally (...) central institution of government' (Mwakyembe, 1985:25).

For example, in order to change Tanganyika to a republic, the National Executive Committee (NEC) of TANU recommended the idea first to the government. The government then presented it to the National Assembly and a motion was subsequently introduced in parliament and passed on 15 February, 1962, (Mwakyembe, 1985).

Secondly, a government paper 'Proposal of the Tanganyika Government for a Republic' was prepared. The prime minister referred the paper to the National Assembly noting the position of the National Assembly in the government system. He referred to it as [3]

> ...the voice of the nation and fount of authority which must remain sovereign. (...) 'if the proposals contained in this white paper are approved by the National Assembly at this sitting, as I hope they will be, legislative provision will be made at this sitting of the Assembly for the President-Designate of the Republic of Tanganyika, and on December 9th, 1962, Tanganyika will become a Republic within the Commonwealth, (28 June, 1962, Col. 1985 Hansard).

The government white paper was accepted in the National Assembly on 28 June, 1962. The tone of the speech made by Mr Rashidi Mfaume Kawawa, the prime minister, and the process and the sentiments expressed showed that the National Assembly was held in high esteem and reverence.

Parliament between December 1962 and 1965: The republican constitution

On 9 December, 1962, Tanganyika became a republic with a multiparty political system. Apparently the TANU government wanted to avoid the embarrassment of moving from a United Nations Trust Territory to the proclamation of the Queen of Great Britain, Her Majesty Queen Elizabeth II as 'Queen of Tanganyika' (Mwaikusa, 1995). TANU had rejected her during her independence struggle.

The republic came, however, with a completely new constitution called *the Constitution of Tanganyika, 1962*, often referred to as the Republic Constitution. It changed the structure of power fundamentally, shifting the seat of power from parliament to the executive and especially the presidency. The president took over the powers of the prime minister and the governor-general with the exception of leadership of government business in the National Assembly. This gave him vast powers!

The president was vested with all executive power which was going to be exercised by himself or by a person holding office in the service of the republic. In relation to parliament, the president was not a member of the National Assembly but was a constituent part of *parliament*. He could appoint up to ten members to the National Assembly and address it at any time. He could dissolve parliament at any time but he had no powers to prorogue it. This meant that he could not dismiss parliament without dissolving it because this would have meant his remaining in power. Dissolving it entailed his going out of office also.

In his relationship to the executive, the President appointed a vice-president (VP) from among elected members of parliament. He also determined the number of ministries without any reference to parliament as had been the case under the independence constitution. He could remove the VP and ministers at any time. Closely connected to this, the president had a lot of powers with regard to the bureaucracy. He could create offices and appoint, fire, promote or discipline those he appointed. The Civil Service Commission did the work for him, basing their powers on the Civil Service Act, 1962.

For the judiciary, he appointed the chief justice and other judges of the High Court, but could not dismiss them. The Judicial Service Commission appointed other officers of the judiciary for the president.

But as with the Civil Service Commission, the members of Judicial Service Commission were appointed by the president. The Director of Public Prosecutions lost his independence and security of tenure. The exercise of his power became subject to the directions of the president.

On top of combining the offices of the prime minister and the governor-general, the constitution gave him powers to ignore parliament and everybody else (The Constitution of Tanganyika 1962, op. cit. Article 3 (3))

> '.....in the exercise of his functions, the President shall act in his own discretion and shall not be obliged to follow advice tendered by any other person.'

The control functions over the executive were thus severely cut down. The independence constitution had required the cabinet to be collectively responsible to parliament for the conduct of government. The government could be removed from office by a parliamentary vote of no confidence. *The Constitution of Tanganyika 1962* did not provide for this. The cabinet was in fact responsible to the president as the constitution provided (Ibid. Article 11 (3))

> 'The Vice-President and the other Ministers shall be responsible under the direction of the President for such departments of state or other business of the government as the President may assign them.'

It was only the president who could hold the ministers responsible for their actions. But since the president was not a member of the National Assembly, the government was indeed not accountable to parliament (Mwaikusa, 1995). The preamble of the republican constitution stated that Tanganyika was a 'democratic society responsible and answerable to the people'.

Given the fact that preambles of constitutions are not part of the constitutions, the statement had no force of law. Over and above these vast powers, the president had added powers from colonial laws. He could deport people from one part of the country to another and he could 'expel' undesirables under another ordinance. He could declare an emergency, etc.

The republican constitution took away from the National Assembly the weapon to control the action of the executive by a vote of no confidence. The assembly could have recourse to a laborious and long drawn process of confrontation with the executive if the president refused to assent to a bill. The showdown could lead to a dissolution of parliament, the resignation of the president and the calling of new elections.

The steps to be followed were as follows:
(i) The president would refuse to assent to a bill after which he had to return it to the assembly with the reason(s) for his refusal to sign. The bill could not be presented to the president again for assent within six months.
(ii) If the assembly insisted on its being signed, it could return it to the president for assent within six months but with two thirds majority support of the bill by the MPs.
(iii) The president was obliged to sign the re-passed bill within 21 days or dissolve parliament. The dissolution implied his own resignation and the calling of new elections.

Besides being confrontational and long drawn, the process was fraught with danger for the MPs themselves because even the most popular MPs had to be nominated by their party before they could contest their seats. The support of the president of their party, who was the president of the country, would most probably not materialise if the popular MPs had differences with their president. In all likelihood the MPs would avoid following this route to 'discipline' their executive. All these points show that in fact parliament was on its way to a decline.

The year 1962 saw also the decline of parliament vis-a-vis the party because, although the new constitution did not change the position of parliament vis-a-vis the party, TANU was in total control because the executive and the president were all members of TANU. There was a *de facto* one party situation, which gave further powers to the president.

The proposal to make the powers of the president vast was opposed by at least three members of the independence parliament namely Mr Herman Sarwatt, who was an independent MP, Mr Tunze and Mr Mtaki warning that the enormous powers could easily be misused and that the sovereignty of parliament was at stake. The argument was that leaders come and go while the constitution would be there for 'years to come' (Parliamentary Debates, June 28, 1962, Cols, 1096 and 1101).

The prime minister in June 1962 was Mr Rashidi Mfaume Kawawa as Mr Julius Nyerere had resigned in January, 1962, and become a backbencher. Nyerere, however, defended those vast powers. He emphasised the need for having what he called a 'National Ethic' which would be the only 'safeguard of a people's right, the people's freedom and those things which they value'. The key emphasis was leaders having the spirit of refusing things 'un-Tanganyikan', having leaders who would not *act in an insane way*. (Ibid. Cols 1103-1114) He underscored the use of powers under the constitution but also being able to build the National ethic and to refuse things not good for the country (Ibid.)

> 'What we must continue to do all the time is to build an ethic of this nation, which makes the Head of State, whoever he is to say, "I have the power to do this under the Constitution, but I cannot do it, it is un-Tanganyikan.' Or for the people of Tanganyika, if they have made a mistake and elected an insane individual as their Head of State, who has the power under the constitution to do X, Y and Z if he tried to do it, the people of Tanganyika would say, "We won't have it from anybody, President or President squared, we won't have it. I believe, Sir, that is the way we ought to look at this constitution"'.

It is argued that parliament accepted the new constitution because members knew that the first president was going to be Nyerere. Opposing him or doubting his wisdom and ability would not have sounded right. 'It was his personality which alleviated fears of likely misuse of powers by the President.' (Mwaikusa, 1995: 92). There is, however, a contradiction in logic. Indeed, one cannot fail to note the faulty logic in Nyerere's reasoning. If the constitution was giving the Tanganyikan president powers, which he would deem un-Tanganyikan to use because he had the spirit of the national ethic, why then did that same constitution have to give this very ethical Tanganyikan president those powers?

There was also a lot of idealism in Nyerere's argumentation. He assumed that people would act against an insane head of state who had all constitutional powers. But, unfortunately the people had no organs for use in the confrontation.

In the end Nyerere had to appeal to faith - *kuaminiana*. (Parliamentary Debates, June 28, 1962.)

> "We have got to have a little amount of faith, although I know that some Members have been questioning this idea of faith. But, Sir, democracy is a declaration of faith in human nature, the very thing we are struggling to safeguard here, the very idea of democracy is a declaration of faith in mankind. And every enemy of democracy, is some person who somewhere has no faith in human beings. He doubts. He thinks *he* is right, but other human beings are not all right. *He* will be perfectly alright".

It would seem to us that Nyerere here was in fact appealing to the members of parliament to have faith in him.

Parliament under the Interim Constitution: Struggle for supremacy between the executive and the party on the one hand and parliament on the other

The Interim Constitution came immediately after two very far reaching events in the political life of Tanganyika, namely (i) the Union of Tanganyika and Zanzibar and (ii) the institution of the one party state. It was "interim" because a new permanent constitution was supposed to be written and passed within one year. It came twelve years later!

The Interim Constitution was presented to the National Assembly on 8 June, 1965, and adopted by the Constituent Assembly on 11 July, 1965, one month later. There was no government motion to the National Assembly and no government white paper as had happened with the steps to becoming a republic (Mwaikusa, 1995).

The provisions of the Interim Constitution remained basically like those of the Republican Constitution except for three areas: (a) enshrining the one party in the constitution; (ii) changing election procedures and (c) fundamentally changing the composition of parliament. Whereas the Republican Constitution had created an executive president who was part of the legislature but not accountable to it, the interim constitution raised the party to a new constitutional position. The executive stabilised its position of dominance. Parliament on the other hand began to lose its legislative supremacy.

For example, in January 1967, the NEC of TANU adopted the Arusha Declaration. This was a major policy shift which was supposed to be passed by parliament. It was not debated there. The Arusha Declaration in 1967, was used as the basis for announcing the nationalisation of the major means of production and exchange which were thought to be essential to socialism, starting with banks, insurance and a few factories and followed later by plantations and farms which were nationalised later. Parliament was not involved in all this.

Parliament was made to act *post factum* to give retrospective legal force to the nationalisation as happened on 14 and 15 February, 1967, when it met and passed the necessary laws. (the National Bank of Commerce (Establishment and Vesting of Assets and Liabilities) Act 1967, the State Trading Corporation (Establishment and Vesting of Interests Act., 1967), the National Agricultural Products Board (Vesting of Interest) Act, 1967, the Insurance (Vesting of Interests and Regulations) Act 1967 and the Industrial Shares (Acquisition) Act 1967. Given the situation, parliament could not reject the bills. Parliament had thus changed from a legislating authority to a rubber stamp giving legitimacy to decisions made elsewhere. This further signified the decline of parliament.

Furthermore, in terms of function, the party and especially the NEC within its structures, became more and more important in many ways:
- Members of the NEC of TANU who were not MPs were henceforth going to be paid as MPs (Mlimuka and Kabudi, 1985).
- The Interim Constitution gave the NEC the power to select electoral candidates. Since they also had the final say in expelling party members who, if they were MPs would lose their seats, parliament was made responsible to the NEC.
- The NEC was given the privilege of summoning witnesses and calling for papers as the National Assembly had.
- The principal secretary to the president (i.e. the head of the Civil Service) and the attorney general were made members of NEC' as they (were) of the National Assembly (...) in order for NEC to be aware of the administrative and legal implications of the policies it was formulating' (MacAuslan and Ghai, 1972:203).

- Even more significantly, the constitution of TANU became an annex of the state constitution as a schedule. Mwaikusa (1995) argues that since TANU could change its constitution at will, the party was authorised (in effect) to dictate amendments to the constitution of the state by this measure.

The following examples of constitutional changes through the party signify this move. The Arusha Declaration, for example, adopted a strict leadership code for people holding political and administrative offices. TANU and government leaders, including Members of Parliament, were prohibited from having shares in capitalist companies, owning houses for rental, having two salaries, and being directors in private companies. The Interim Constitution was thus amended to require all MPs to comply with them. They were given a year and one month i.e. 13 months after 5 February, 1967, to have complied with the provisions.

The other example given is that the government implemented socialism in 1967 with its concomitant nationalisations 'without waiting for a Presidential Commission on Socialism' (Mwaikusa, 1995: 134) which should have been the route under normal circumstances. In 1968, MPs were sacked by the party. This was another example of the dominance of NEC. Finally, all major policy decisions had to be submitted to the NEC first for consideration and approval *before* being taken to the National Assembly, for example the Five Year Plans of 1965 and 1969 and Decentralisation in 1972.

As we pointed out above, the composition of the National Assembly was one other indicator of how parliament could exercise its supervisory role over the executive and thus clearly manifest the sovereignty of parliament as an instrument for controlling government. The interim constitution weakened the National Assembly in this aspect in two major ways: (a) it robbed it of its powers to censor the executive. The executive thus remained totally unchecked. (b) The president got powers to appoint a large number of MPs and from among them some ministers.

The republican constitution had allowed the president to appoint up to ten MPs. The Interim Constitution allowed him to appoint many more as follows:

- 10 MPs allowed earlier by the Republican Constitution.
- 32 Members of the Revolutionary Council;
- 20 MPs to represent Zanzibar. They were appointed by the president in consultation with the first vice president; and
- 20 regional commissioners ex-officio but appointed by the president initially as regional commissioners.

This brought the total of presidential appointees to eighty-two. With a House comprising 204 members of whom 107 were elected from constituencies and fifteen indirectly, the president appointed slightly over 40 per cent of the assembly (Mwaikusa, 1995). It is not hard to imagine that these appointees would toe the executive line. After all, they were responsible to the president.

The president at times used these powers to put back into the National Assembly persons who had been rejected at the poll. For example, Paul Bomani was appointed to parliament and to the cabinet, becoming Minister of Finance after he had been defeated at the polls in 1965; Johnston Kihampa was defeated in 1970. He was made regional commissioner and therefore *ex-officio* MP; Daudi Mwakawago lost his seat in 1980. He was appointed MP. in 1981 and became a cabinet minister in 1982; the saga of Chrisant Mzindakaya makes even more spellbinding reading. He won his parliamentary seat in the elections of 1980 but lost it after a petition in 1981. He contested the by-election and lost, but he was returned to parliament as an *ex-officio* MP after his appointment as regional commissioner (Mwaikusa, 1995). Would or could such MPs who had been accorded a favour to return to parliament, be critical of the executive? We are inclined to answer in the negative!

It would seem that Zanzibari nominated MPs, especially from the Revolutionary Council, could have their tenure stopped by being relieved of their positions on the Revolutionary Council. Mrs Milembe Ng'winamila, MP for Geita South, complained in 1968 of seeing new faces from Zanzibar during every session without the august House being informed of the fate of former MPs, suggesting that MPs took seats without being sworn in. If this had been done the MP would have had no cause to complain! Even the reluctance from Zanzibar MPs to criticise the government indicated fear of their appointments being revoked if they spoke their minds.

Parliament's attempts to assert itself: 1968 and 1973

Members of parliament did not take the encroachment on the powers of parliament in silence. They questioned which organ was more supreme the parliament or the party? (Hansard 18 Julym, 1967, question No. 500; (P. Msekwa, 1978:40; Mwakyembe op. 41). The question was played down by the government but came up again in 1968 during the budget session.

There was a proposition that one of the articles which spelled out the president's powers be amended to provide for the National Assembly to be 'constitutionally the advisor of the President' of Tanzania (Van Velzen and Sterkenburg, 1972: 249) The president would then be obliged to act only on the advice of the national assembly which he averred was 'supreme.' The argument was that any matter which might be initially considered by any other organ, such as TANU or the cabinet, should ultimately be submitted to the national assembly for final approval or other action. This was argued to be the right kind of democracy for Tanzania and no other arrangement was 'democratic.'

Mr Rashidi Mfaume Kawawa, the second Vice President and leader of government business in the national assembly, strongly supported TANU and the ASP as supreme organs and urged MPs disagreeing with that arrangement to quit. He menacingly gave notice that the NEC would screen certain MPs. This was in contradiction to the call from 'the same vice-president who only two weeks earlier had urged the MPs to speak openly and without fear even if they were critical of the Government.' Minister Aboud Jumbe complained 'bitterly' that Zanzibar had been brought to trial by the unfair criticism of the MPs.

In the October 1968, session of parliament there were complaints raised again that there were too many nominated members. The following demands were made:
- the National Assembly should have a large majority of elected members;
- three quarters of the president's powers should be vested in parliament;
- there should be two or more parties;
- there should be two candidates in presidential elections;
- there should be elections in Zanzibar;

- ASP chairpersons should not have magisterial powers in Zanzibar; and finally.
- Between parliament and TANU, it was parliament which was supreme.
- (*Hansard.* 1 October 1968: cols 30-42; *The Standard*, Dar es Salaam: Tanganyika Newspapers Ltd., 2 October, 1968.)

Those who argued for party supremacy emphasised in no uncertain terms the following the among other things: the supremacy of the party; that all MPs were expected to work under the leadership of the party, that the party could discipline MPs and that parliament belonged to TANU. It was categorically stated that the party was supreme and was 'the vanguard of the revolution [a point which had to] be understood once and for all'. Ibid. cols 47-48.

Some two weeks later, the NEC demonstrated its supremacy by expelling the critical MPs from TANU for what it termed 'gross violation of the party creed and opposition to its policies' (Van Velzen and Sterkenburg, 1972: 248). Thrown out of the party were the following: G. Kaneno (Karagwe), T. Bakampenja (Ihangiro), J. Kasella-Bantu (Nzega East), S. Kibuga (Mufindi), M. Chogga (Iringa South), F. Masha (Geita East) and W. Mwakitwange (National). NEC also used the occasion to expel two other prominent members, namely Oscar S. Kambona (Morogoro East) and Eli Anangisye (Rungwe North). Mr Kambona, a former Cabinet Minister, Secretary General of TANU and close confidant of Nyerere had gone into self-imposed exile to Britain. Eli Anangisye was a former Secretary General of the TANU Youth League. They were expelled from the party because they allegedly 'tried to subvert the TANU Government [and] did not believe in TANU nor its socialist ideology' *The Nationalist editorial* 21 October, 1968.

According to several articles of the Interim Constitution, when read together, the expelled party members also lost their parliamentary seats because, to become an MP, a person had to be a party member first. If a sitting MP lost any of the qualifications which qualified him to become an MP he lost the seat automatically. These early battles were thus lost by the MPs.

It is worth noting that the happenings of October 1968, demonstrated that parliament was no longer the sovereign and revered institution, as was the case in 1962. In the opinion of many analysts, it had lost much of its public esteem. It was no longer an important national institution if its members could have such severe punishment meted out to them for exercising their rights of free speech in the House as members.

In spite of its having been superseded by the NEC of TANU and having been relegated to the technical function of passing laws, parliament made two further very notable attempts to assert its authority over the government. One was part of the 1968 struggles recounted above while the other took place in 1973.

During the July 1968 parliamentary session, a private member's motion was tabled by Mr James Paul Ndobho (Musoma North) urging the government to abandon its intention of granting ministers, regional and area commissioners very generous gratuities contrary to the spirit of the Arusha Declaration. Although the decision to make those grants seems to have come from the president himself, the motion was carried.

The second attempt came in 1973, again under the leadership of Mr James Paul Ndobho. Whereas in 1968, the Ndobho motion had been supported by a few MPs, this time around, the majority of the members of parliament rejected the Income Tax Bill which the government wanted to pass into law in November 1973. The president had to exercise his right to address the National Assembly at any time he wanted. In his address, he threatened the MPs with the dissolution of parliament if they chose to continue to reject the Finance Bill before them. With this threat hanging above them, the MPs meekly passed the bill *unanimously* into law when it was brought before them for deliberation soon afterwards.

Parliament proved to be powerless in face of the executive. This marked the end of its attempt to assert its authority for the time being! Ndobho was 'exiled' to Moscow as ambassador!

Further descent into powerlessness

One of the indications of the position of parliament in the body politic is its composition. By 1975, the composition of parliament was such that the representative character of that institution was almost lost. A constitutional amendment reduced the number of directly elected constituency members of parliament from 120 to 88. The number was soon after raised to 96. At the same time, as the number of directly elected constituency members was decreased, the number of indirectly elected members was increased from 20 to 35.

According to the 1975 law, there was going to be one MP per district. It was stated that his role was not to represent people in the district, but to be a member of a leadership team, a *troika* with the TANU district chairman and secretary of TANU as the other members. There were going to be 'national MPs' and 'Regional MPs.' Of 218 members of parliament, only 96 were elected. This meant that a *minority* of the members were *real* representatives of the people (44.04 per cent).

The 1977 Constitution: The *nadir* of parliamentary decline

In 1975, members of parliament lost, to a certain extent, their representative character. But the real crunch, its *nadir*, came at the time when parliament lost its supremacy to the party constitutionally. It was made a committee of the *Chama cha Mapinduzi* (CCM), the party which was born on 5 Februrary, 1977, after the merger of TANU and ASP. The party constitution stated that all MPs were a committee of the National Conference. The committee's function was to make sure that party policies were implemented.

The composition of the National Assembly indicates the continuation of the trend begun in 1975. It had the following members in 1977:

(a)	The Union vice-president (ex-officio)	1
(b)	Directly elected constituency members	111
(c)	Indirectly elected national members from candidates nominated by mass organisations	15
(d)	Indirectly elected national members from the regions (Elected by the assembly)	25
(e)	Regional commissioners (ex-officio)	25
(f)	Indirectly elected national members (by the Zanzibar House of Representatives)	32
(g)	National members from Zanzibar appointed by the president	20
(h)	National members appointed by the president from the mainland	10
	Total	**239**

There was a total of 128 members of parliament who were not elected directly by the people. Those appointed by the president numbered 55. Both figures indicated the powerlessness of parliament then because of the indirectly elected members. *Maybe* only those from the mass organisations could speak freely in the House or act against the executive. The rest were to all intents and purposes the 'President's men.' But then, even members from mass organisations had their freedom curtailed by the fact that the organisations were institutions of the ruling party!

Parliament had no more constitutional control over legislation. It hadn't even indirect constitutional control over the actions of the executive as had been the case at independence. It became a rubber stamp of party and executive decisions. The most glaring and often quoted example occurred at the end of 1982, when, during a live New Year message to the nation over Radio Tanzania, among other things, Nyerere announced new tax measures (*Daily News*, Dar es Salaam, 1 January, 1983.)

> You will already have heard of the new taxes which come into force tomorrow, the first of January, 1983. *'These tax measures will be debated in parliament in its next sitting, but in the meantime they have to be paid by everyone.'* (Emphasis added).

The president seems to have been sure that parliament would endorse the new taxes, further showing how parliament was reduced to such low straits thus losing its relevance. Tax measures proposed by the executive have to be enacted as legislation by parliament. This example of taxation by the executive, meant legislation by the executive.

Other examples of the work of parliament being done by other bodies abound. Unlike, for example, the procedure which was followed in 1962 to draft the Republican Constitution, in 1977, the twenty member committee which drafted the CCM Constitution was given the job to look into the Interim Constitution and propose changes or draft a new one. The committee was appointed as a Constitutional Commission on 16 March, 1977, long after it had started its work and shortly before it submitted its proposals to NEC. There was no government motion to parliament (Mwaikusa, 1995).

In 1981, the NEC of the CCM sacked Minister Augustine Mwingira and ATC General Manager Mmasi for gross mishandling of aircraft purchases. In January 1984, the NEC censored Vice-President Aboud Jumbe and dismissed him as party Vice-Chairman and Vice-President. This should have been the work of parliament under normal circumstances. The work of parliament had been taken over by the NEC of the party, as pointed out above, in a process known as party supremacy. This process had begun in 1965, was stressed in parliament in 1968 and became law in 1975. In 1977, it became part of the constitution. The president was directed to always abide by the policies and directives of the party.

The position parliament found itself in was contradictory and therefore unenviable. If the major tasks of the National Assembly were to give legislative force to party policies and act as a watchdog over the activities of government, there is no way it could do this without having opinions on the policies themselves. But too vigorous open criticism by MPs could lead to clashes with the superior body, the NEC. MacAuslan and Ghai are of the opinion that as a result of this situation hot discussions tended to be held at committee stage where open criticism was allowed, at least in the early seventies, for policies of minor importance because 'holders of power dislike being criticised; if they are wise, they would invite criticism, but prefer it to be in private, unless they have a positive incentive to favour public discussion' (MacAuslan and Ghai, 1972: 205) However, these authors continue to note that there was no positive incentive to make public criticism. Since it seems that '*private* debates in party organs (were) rigorous and effective in changing ministerial viewpoints and government policies, the arrangement appeared to both sides to be satisfactory.' But the end result was that parliament remained mum.

Constitutional changes in 1984: The Fifth Constitutional Amendment

In 1983, CCM initiated a debate on the Constitution. Between February and September 1983, over 9,335 proposals from all over the country were received by the CCM in Dodoma. Many proposed sweeping changes.

For purposes of this chapter we will look at areas affecting parliament and the president. We can say in general that parliament *began* to regain its supremacy as the organ of state representing all the people, their rights and interests with the fifth constitutional amendment of 1984.

In terms of *composition,* the National Assembly became more representative: directly elected members *increased* from the 111 of 1977 to 169. Indirectly elected decreased from 72 to 35 and the number of those appointed by the president fell from 56 to 40. This figure included regional commissioners. (Constitution of Tanzania 1977, Article 66)

The indirectly elected members were: 15 women, 15 members from five mass organisations (three from each) and five members elected by the Zanzibar House of Representatives (Ibid., Articles 78 to 80.) Elected members constituted 69.25 per cent of all members. Those appointed by the president constituted only 16.4 per cent. This was a huge change!

In terms of *function* a new Article was introduced which stated clearly that *Ibid.*, Article 63 (2)

> 'The National Assembly shall be the principal organ of the United Republic which shall, on behalf of the people, supervise and advise the government of the United Republic and all its agencies in the exercise of their functions in accordance with this constitution.'

It is clear here that parliament was regaining its supervisory and control role. It was also regaining its supremacy as an organ of representation.

Another article made ministers responsible to the National Assembly. *Ibid.* Article 53 (2).

> The Ministers, led by the Prime Minister, shall be collectively responsible to the National Assembly for the discharge of the functions of the Government of the United Republic.

They were, however, also responsible to the president by virtue of his being the appointing authority.

In terms of *operation*, parliament was protected by a new article which made parliamentary proceedings absolutely privileged and not to be questioned anywhere outside parliament. This article was reinforced by a law which stated that (a) speeches made in parliament could not be questioned in court, (b) MPs were free to organise meetings in their constituencies and (c) respective authorities in the districts were enjoined to facilitate the holding of such meetings.

It must be noted, however, that, although its composition and status changed for the better, the National Assembly did not get back its powers to pass a motion of no confidence in the prime minister. It also remained a 'special committee of the National Conference of the Party' for the purpose of supervising the implementation of party policies by the government and parastatal organisations. This was also a significant change because the purposes were specific. They were *not* stated in general terms.

The enhancement of the powers of the National Assembly went along with the enhancement of the role of the judiciary and some changes in the powers of the president. His discretionary powers were now subject to the supremacy of the law and *not* that of the *party*. His tenure was limited to only two terms of five years each. He appointed a prime minister and in consultation with him, the cabinet of ministers.

It is important to note that (a) party supremacy was slightly limited. Whereas previously it had been supreme according to its own constitution, in 1984 it remained supreme with 'final authority in respect of all matters (...) subject to this constitution and party constitution'. It was also stated that the executive under the president determined the general policy of the government.

However, in practice, party supremacy still remained because the president was the chairman of the party. (b) The principle of separation of powers was declared. This was a new thing in the constitution. All state authority was vested in the three separate organs of state: the legislature, the executive and the judiciary. The three organs were required to exercise their functions according to the constitution. This amendment does, to some great extent, signify the change in the leadership pattern, particularly the anticipated changes in the presidency and a strong move away from having 'faith in mankind' to a belief in a written constitution as the best safeguard of people's rights.

The Constitutional Amendments of 1992: More Power to parliament

The Presidential Commission on the One Party or Multiparty System in Tanzania chaired by Chief Justice Francis Lukas Nyalali recommended among other things, that Tanzania abandon the one party system and follows the multiparty system. This change required far reaching changes in the constitution.

Many salient articles were changed which touched on the power and sovereignty of parliament. They included:

(i) Removal of sections of the article which had made Tanzania a one party state with the CCM as the final authority. Tanzania was declared to be a 'democratic and socialist' state with a multiparty political system.

(ii) Repeal of articles which had given the CCM monopoly over political activity.

(iii) Repeal of constitutional provisions requiring the president to observe 'the policies and objectives of the party'.

(vi) Repeal of the article which had made the National Assembly 'a committee of the National Conference of the Party'.

(v) Repeal of provisions giving the NEC of CCM or any other organs state responsibilities.

As far as the composition of the National Assembly was concerned, regional commissioners ceased to be ex-officio members of the House. The president no longer appointed members of parliament. The only member allowed was the attorney general (AG) who entered the House in that capacity. The number of constituencies and their boundaries were to be determined from time to time by the National Electoral Commission with the approval of the president.

For the October 1995 elections, there were to be 220 constituencies with the National Assembly looking as follows:

(i) Directly elected constituency members   220
(ii) Indirectly elected members by the Zanzibar
    House of Representatives from among their members   5
(iii) Indirectly elected women representatives   15
(iv) The Attorney General (ex-officio)   1
    Total   **241**

This was a very high proportion of elected members after very many years.

The ninth amendment to the constitution enacted in December 1992 made even more significant changes as far as parliament was concerned:
- The National Assembly could impeach the president if he acted against the constitution or acted in a manner bringing disrepute to the Office of the President.

The process of impeachment required a notice for a motion of impeachment. This notice has to be supported by at least 20 per cent of the M.Ps. It has to be submitted to the speaker at least 30 days before representation to the assembly. If two thirds of the assembly vote in favour of the motion, a special committee of enquiry is formed headed by the chief justice and consisting of the chief justice of Zanzibar and seven MPs appointed by the speaker.

The nine member committee then investigates the accusations made against the president who is given a hearing. It reports to the speaker within 90 days. The National Assembly discusses the report giving the president another hearing. It then votes. If it is resolved by a two thirds majority to remove the president, he is removed from power. If removed by impeachment, a president loses all his retirement benefits as well as his immunity from court proceedings enjoyed normally by him as per provision of the constitutions of 1977.

(i) One is bound to note that the procedures for the impeachment of the president are so difficult that it is almost impossible to impeach him. Maybe it is good that it remains so because if casual procedures to impeach the president are followed, the president might be inhibited in the exercise of his powers after he has been democratically elected.

(ii) The article which had empowered the president to 'dissolve parliament at any time' was removed. It was replaced by provisions setting out circumstances in which he could dissolve parliament.

The circumstances for the dissolution of parliament are:

(a) Refusal by the National Assembly to pass the annual budget of the government;

(b) When a bill already refused assent by the president is sent back to him for signature within six months of refusal and with a two-thirds majority of MPs supporting it;

(c) When the government is defeated on an important motion concerning basic policy;
(d) When the government loses its majority support in the National Assembly;
(e) At any time during the last twelve months of the life of parliament. But in this case the president must not be under impeachment proceedings.

(iii) The National Assembly got back power to censure the government by passing a resolution of no confidence in the prime minister. The procedures for this included starting with a notice supported by 20 per cent of MPs. The notice must be submitted to the speaker at least 14 days before it is presented to the assembly. No special committee is instituted but the motion is debated straight away and the motion is carried by only a simple majority. The prime minister must thereafter resigns within two days of the resolution. When he vacates his office, all the other ministers must vacate their offices with him.

This article has restored the collective responsibility of the prime minister and other ministers to the National Assembly. There is still a weakness because the full cabinet includes the president and his vice-president who are not members of the National Assembly.

(iv) The president is enjoined by Article 51 to appoint a prime minister from among elected constituency MPs only. The PM must belong to the party having or likely to have a majority in the House. This appointment must be approved by the National Assembly.

All these provisions have enhanced the power of Parliament immensely and made it truly the supreme state institution exercising control and supervisory functions over government activities.

The Eleventh Constitution Amendment Act of 1994 introduced the system of having a 'running-mate' to obtain a vice-president. He is therefore no longer appointed by the president and cannot be removed by him. He can be removed only by impeachment, for which purpose also the president can initiate proceedings. If the presidency falls vacant the VP automatically becomes president for the remainder of the term. He, as the new president, appoints a new VP who must be approved by the National Assembly.

Conclusion

Let us conclude by noting first that, although the National Assembly has become very powerful now, it stands facing a president who is still extremely powerful. He retains full powers over the civil service: he can create and abolish offices and he can hire and fire civil servants down up to the lowest levels. He can also still act without listening to anyone's advice.

Secondly, although parliament may have regained its former competence to the level it had in 1962, it will have to prove itself operationally in future, especially in the areas of exercising its control functions. It will have to face the Herculean task of limiting the profligacy of the executive arm of the state by coming to grips with corruption in the civil service and the police. It will also have to deal with a very corrupt judiciary.

References

Cliffe, Lionel and Saul, John S, (eds) (1972). *Socialism in Tanzania, An Interdisciplinary Reader, Vol. I: Politics*, Nairobi: East African Publishing House.

Cliffe, Lionel, (1972) "Democracy in a One-Party State: The Tanzanian Experience" in Ibid., pp. 241-247.

Government of Tanganyika (1961). *Legislative Council Debates*, Dar es Salaam: Government Printer.

Government of Tanganyika (1962). *Parliament Debates,*: Dar es Salaam: Government Printer.

Government of Tanzania (1968). *Majadiliano ya Bunge,*: Dar es Salaam: Government Printer

Government of Tanzania (1992). *Tume ya Rais ya Mfumo wa Chama Kimoja au Vyama Vingi vya Siasa Tanzania, 1991, Taarifa ya Mapendekezo ya Tume Kuhusu Mfumo wa Siasa Nchini Tanzania*, Dar es Salaam.

McAuslan, J.P.W.B. and Ghai, Yash,(1972) 'Constitutional Innovation and Political Stability in Tanzania' in Cliffe, L. and Saul, John S., (eds), pp.248-253.

Mlimuka, Aggrey K.L.J. and Kabudi, Palamagamba J.A.M., (1985) "The State and the Party", in Shivji, Issa G., (ed.), 57-86.

Mwaikusa, Jwani Timothy, (1995). 'Towards Responsible Democratic Government', D. Phil. Dissertation, London SOAS.

Mwakyembe, Harrison G., (1985). *'The Parliament and the Electoral Process'*, in Shivji, Issa G. (ed.): 16-56.

Pratt, R. Cranford, (1972). 'The Cabinet and Presidential Leadership in Tanzania in 1960-66' in Cliffe, L. and Saul, John S. (eds): 226-240.

Shivji, Issa G (ed.) (1985). *The State and the Working People in Tanzania*, Dakar: Codesria.

Stephens, H.W., (1968). *The Political Transformation of Tanganyika: 1920-67*, New York: Praeger.

Van Velzen, H.U.E. Thoden and Sterkenburg, J.J., (1972). *'Stirrings in the Tanzanian National Assembly'* in Cliffe, L. and Saul, John S. (eds): 248-253.

Van Velzen, H.U.E. Thoden and Sterkenburg, J.J., (1972). *'The Party Supreme'* in Cliffe, L. and Saul, John S., (eds): 257-264.

5

The General Environment in which the Members of Parliament Work

Charles Gasarasi

Introduction

This chapter attempts to examine the general environment in which the member of parliament in Tanzania discharges his/her functions as a representative of the people. The underlying assumption is that Tanzania is a 'liberal' democratic system in the making and that its parliament is the basis for the country's representative government. Thus, the elected member of parliament is perceived as the representative of his/her constituency. Such representation has been defined by Carl J. Friedrich (1968:278) as:

> '...the process by and through which the political power and influence which the entire citizenry or a part of them might have upon governmental action is, with their express or implied approval, exercised on their behalf by a small number among them, with binding effect upon the whole community thus represented.'

There are multiple functions that an effective member of parliament is expected to engage in as a representative of his/her constituency. Mushi (this volume) has outlined the most salient of such functions at three hierarchical levels: the national, constituency and personal levels.

National level functions include: law-making; passing and amending the constitution; approving taxes, other revenues and budgets; making or shaping public policy; controlling government actions; informing government about constituency situation; resource allocation nationally; and providing leadership nationally.

Constituency-level functions include: informing constituency about government actions; plans and policies; helping to settle conflicts and resolve grievances of constituents; aggregating and articulating interests of constituents to relevant authorities; resource allocation locally; mobilising efforts for development of constituency and providing leadership locally.

Personal-level functions include: self-advertising; credit claiming; and position taking. These functions are meant to fetch fame and a good image for the member of parliament who wants to become a successful career politician.

The member of Parliament's success or failure in performing the above functions largely depends on the nature of the obtaining environment, conceptualised by Mushi (this volume) as the nature of the prevailing structural, cultural and economic factors.

Structural factors mainly refer to the political structure itself such as: the political system; the party system; the electoral system; the parliament type; power distribution among the three branches of government, power distribution in society and the state of civil society.

Cultural factors mainly refer to the nature of the prevailing political culture including: political competence of the citizenry; the MP's perception of his/her role and power and expectations from constituents.

Economic factors refer to availability or lack of financial, human, logistical and other resources necessary to enable the member of parliament to fulfill his/her functions efficiently and effectively.

The above factors, either singly or in combination, are perceived as major parts of an environment which may constrain or facilitate the work of a member of parliament in his/her functions as an elected representative of Tanzania's citizenry.

In the following sections of this chapter, we first attempt to discuss the extent to which the Tanzanian political system may help or impede the member of parliament's representative functions. Secondly, we discuss some survey data in relation to the work environment of members of parliament. We finally comment on the resource environment within which members of parliament discharge their representative functions.

The political system structure as a work environment for the member of parliament

The political system structure of Tanzania has changed several times since the independence of Tanganyika in 1961. These changes have also invariably changed the work environment of representatives of the people in the legislature. The five different constitutions under which the country was ruled from 1961 to 1977 eloquently illustrate the changing nature of the said environment.

The political system

At independence in 1961, Tanganyika became a unitary state under a Westminster constitutional model with provisions for multiparty democracy and parliamentary supremacy. However, this parliamentary system was quickly replaced by the presidential system of government, which was introduced by the Republican Constitution of 1962. Yet, even under the country's variant of the presidential system of government, the assembly-cabinet fusion has been maintained to date, a phenomenon which has had significant consequences on the independence of cabinet MPs (who are accountable to the president) and on the relationship between such MPs and their respective constituencies (because the former are less available to the latter). The notion of 'party government' has also been maintained as in the parliamentary system, a phenomenon which has accentuated lack of latitude both on the part of cabinet MPs and ordinary MPs. Under this arrangement, the much-feared party whip has been effective in government and ruling party control over representatives.

The articles of the Union of 1964 and the Interim Constitution of the United Republic of Tanganyika and Zanzibar 1964 further changed the political system a great deal. However, despite the Union, the unitary nature of the state system was maintained. This meant continued centralisation of political power and resources which is also a means to maintain control over representatives. But the most important changes directly related to parliamentary representation were the declaration of Tanganyika as a one-party state under the Interim Constitution of 1965 and the subsequent 1975 Amendment, which declared one party - TANU - to be supreme over all state organs Chama

Cha Mapinduzi (CCM), which replaced TANU and the Afro-Shirazi Party (ASP), inherited the sole and supreme party status under the *Constitution of the United Republic of Tanzania, 1977.*

With the introduction of the one-party state, which lasted until 1992, the environment in which representatives would exercise their functions was severely circumscribed. For example, although the representatives could perform some of the national-level functions such as law-making and approval of taxes and other revenues and budgets, they were constrained by party supremacy in the exercise of other functions. They were, for example, not well placed to make or shape public policy or to control government actions.

Msekwa (1995:76-77) has testified to this reality:

> '...Under the one-party system in Tanzania, Members of Parliament were generally at the periphery of the party's structure and activities. For example, they constituted a small minority in the party's supreme decision making body, the National Conference. They had no specific representation on the National Executive Committee, which makes all important policy decisions of the party between National Conferences and whose decisions parliament was bound to implement by enacting appropriate legislation. Even in his/her own district, which is also his/her constituency, the MP's role was again largely peripheral. He/she was only one among the many members of the various party organs.'

The political system based on the 1977 Constitution also had an in-built logic that curtailed the representatives' ability to successfully perform some of their basic functions. One such function is passing and amending the constitution. This became clear when the G-55 motion was introduced in an attempt to restructure the Union into three governments, instead of two. This motion did not stand a chance, not only because it was tabled in the then one-party parliament, but also because of the existing constitutional encumbrances. Issa Shivji (1996) has argued that not only was it difficult for the G-55 motion to secure a two-thirds majority of both Zanzibar and mainland MPs for the motion to pass, but it would also have been unconstitutional for parliament to pass an amendment of that magnitude without usurping the sovereignty of the people.

In matters of the representatives' freedom of speech and debate under the one- party system, such freedom was granted *de jure* by Article 100 of the 1977 Constitution:

> (1) 'There shall be freedom of speech, debate and procedure in the National Assembly, and that freedom shall not be impeached or questioned by any organ of the United Republic, or in any court or other place outside parliament.'

However, although at the surface this provision encourages the representatives to express dissenting views without suffering consequences outside parliament, it did not shield the maverick representative from the wrath of the party whip inside parliament and certainly not inside the secret workings of the one-party bureaucracy. Under such circumstances, at least some of the representatives must have felt compelled to exercise restraint and self-censorship when discharging their basic function of speaking against government actions where necessary.

Personal-level functions of the representatives such as 'credit claiming' and 'position taking' were not easy to exercise under the one-party system either. Under the one-party system, the party and its government monopolised the role of provider. Political achievements of individuals were characterised as the product of the enabling role played by the party. No parliamentary candidate campaigned on a personal manifesto. All used the same party manifesto. In earlier years, most of the campaign resources were provided by the party and its government. The amount of resources allocated to a representative's constituency was centrally determined and the majority of representatives had no influence in this exercise. Because authority to mobilise resources was so centralised, the representative could not solicit additional resources, say from donors, independently. Because of lack of an independent civil society other than organisations affiliated to the party, the representative had no alternative allies to depend on for embarking on original and creative projects in the constituency. Thus, under the above circumstances, the representative had no room to publicise his/her individuality, which is what a representative's personal-level functions are all about.

The political system within which members of parliament discharged their functions as described above came to an end with the passing of the Political Parties Act No.4 of 1992. However, the one-party parliament did not come to an end until 1995.

This introduction of multipartysm had important implications for parliament and parliamentary representation. Multipartysm implied a great measure of autonomy both for the legislature as an institution and the representative as an individual actor. With regard to the autonomy of the legislature, the Nyalali Report (1991) prescribed the following:

> '...In a multiparty democracy, our parliaments will be required to do their work properly especially that of representing the people. They should supervise the affairs of the government and in this regard, they should not only be, but be seen to be the supreme authority in all government affairs and the country at large.'

Indeed, the multiparty parliament formed in 1995 began showing signs of independence, particularly in the area of making the government accountable and challenging bills tabled by the government. This input came mainly from the opposition MPs. For example, pressure from the opposition resulted in the resignation of cabinet ministers alleged to have been involved in corrupt activities. Under this same parliament, government was forced from the House floor to withdraw its bill on benefits of senior officials and re-introduce it at a subsequent session in a revised form.

As for the autonomy of the individual MP, multipartysm was expected to increase his/her importance in the eyes of the party, because now the political fortunes of the party greatly depended on its candidates' electability. Msekwa (1995:77) had this to say about the changing environment:

> '...Under multipartism [sic], ...the Member of Parliament will be absolutely central to the purposes of any political party. For the good or bad fortunes of each party, including CCM, will depend entirely on the party's showing in parliamentary elections. It is the outcome of those elections which will determine whether the party will be in power or out of power, for the next period of five years.'

The MP's liberation from the total mercy of his/her party stems from this added quality of electability, which depends on the assessment by the electorate and not solely determined by the preference of the party machine.

Under these changed circumstances, the incumbent MP can now advertise himself/herself, claim credit and cautiously take positions on issues in order to establish electability in the constituency. Since the party's fortunes depend on the electability of its candidate, the party can now tolerate the self-advertising MP for selfish corporate interests. This is to say that an incumbent MP need not invest too much in seeking patronage to win party nomination at the next election.

Multipartysm has introduced another redeeming dimension with regard to the parties' grip over their MPs. Since 1995, there have been incumbent MPs mainly from CCM, who failed to get party nomination as candidates. Some of these individuals quickly crossed over to other parties, got nominated and won the elections. This happened in those cases where the electorate felt the candidate was electable, regardless of party affiliation. With regard to opposition parties, an MP who has troubles with his/her party has the option of crossing over to another opposition party to seek nomination at the next elections. Or better still, there is also the option of joining the ruling party, make a public apology for having been the Biblical 'prodigal son,' vehemently renounce and condemn the opposition and, if pardoned, hope to be one of the MPs constitutionally appointed by the president.

The multiparty system has, therefore, empowered representatives to better fulfil two of the three categories of functions of the ideal representative, which Mushi (this volume) has summarised as:

1. Functions based on the views, opinions and interests of the constituents.
2. Functions or activities originating from the representative's own judgment of the situation as well as personal convictions and conscience.
3. Functions or decisions based on consideration of national interest.

With regard to the first category of functions, the centrality of the electability of a party candidate in elections requires that the incumbent MP becomes acceptable to his/her constituents before the next election.

This acceptability can only be attained if the MP is seen to identify with and to advance the interests of the constituents. In order to fulfil this requirement, the party must in its own interest tolerate the self-advertisement of the MP in the constituency, on the one hand, while, on the other hand, the MP, in his/her own interest too, must impress his/her constituents by demonstrating tangible responsiveness and benefits to the constituency.

Empowerment in the second category of functions stems from the generally lessened power of the parties over their representatives, because of the imperative of candidate electability in the overall fortunes of the parties. This hypothetically gives more room to the representative to put his/her judgment, personal convictions and conscience in his/her work. But this is only possible if and when the elected MP officially assumes office, which is not always the case under the current multiparty politics. A case in point is Civic United Front (CUF) boycott of government and parliament, which made 15 CUF MPs for the Union House and 19 representatives for the Isles House abdicate their representative functions for two consecutive parliamentary sessions since the 2000 general elections before getting sacked. In such a situation, some of CUF MPs may have privately believed that they should be representing their constituents, but failed to do so because in this particular matter they were totally at the mercy of their party's position. In this case, they clearly could not have exercised personal judgment, convictions and conscience in a job they were not doing in the first place.

With regard to the MPs' undertaking of functions or decisions based on consideration of the national interest, we strongly doubt whether the multiparty environment has empowered them to better fulfil this category of functions. Whereas during the one-party state system there was a fairly consensual understanding of the 'national interest,' it would seem that at present such consensual understanding cannot be taken for granted.

Multipartyism has completed the death process of the national *'Ujamaa'* ideology, which in many ways had shaped the understanding of the notion of Tanzania's 'national interest.' No other well articulated dominant ideology has emerged that would help to crystallize a consensual perception of what Tanzania's current 'national interest' is.

Some parties in parliament seem to be guided by ill-defined policies not anchored in solid ideologies. As a result, the politics both in and outside parliament have become severely adversarial, particularly between the ruling party and the opposition. There are serious differences over the constitution and other national institutions. There are disagreements over many laws of the land. Faith in the executive branch of government has seriously declined, etc.

Thus, under such circumstances, the general understanding of the 'national interest' is bound to be blurred at best, if not seriously lacking. If this be the case, it is likely that representatives would find it extremely difficult to align their functions and decisions with a nebulous 'national interest,' ill-defined and probably no longer consensual.

Even though the era of multipartysm seems to have improved the representatives' work environment, MPs still face certain constitutional constraints with regard to their tenure of office. For example, an MP cannot 'cross the floor' without automatically losing his/her seat as stipulated under Article 71 of the 1977 Constitution. This binds the representative to stick to his/her party for the entire period of the parliament's term. Another constraint is that an MP loses his/her seat the moment he/she is expelled from the party. This shows that the representative's recently gained relief from party control still remains insufficient. This may be the Achilles heel of some from among CUF's MPs who cannot assume the representative office, even if individually they may wish to do so.

The foregoing discussion boils down to the following observations. The work environment of the MP as a representative of the people has undergone changes as the country's political system itself has changed. Under the one-party system, the environment was severely constrained as the MP was totally subjugated by the powerful single party and the executive branch of its government. Thus, the representative had to be subservient to both party and government in his/her functions. His/her major function was to inform his/her constituents about party and government actions, plans and policies. If he/she behaved well, a five-year tenure of office was assured even if he/she did not serve the constituency well. Then, as is still the case today, the electorate had no right to recall a useless representative before the next election.

Under the multiparty system, the environment has become more enabling, particularly because of the relative independence the system offers the MP. For example, an incumbent MP can now seek re-election through a different party. He/she can now mobilise resources for his/her constituency from diverse sources other than the government (from foreign donors, NGOs and local businessmen for example). He/she can even raise his/her own campaign money and venture into self-advertisement beyond the formal party manifesto.

Legislation passed in the multiparty era has further liberated the MPs, as a collective body, from the tight control of the executive. For example, although the president still has the powers to dissolve parliament, such powers have been a bit reduced by the Ninth Constitutional Amendment Act of 1992. In addition, parliament has been granted the legal weapon of impeaching against the president under certain circumstances.

It can, therefore, be said that today, the MP enjoys a better work environment than that of the era of the one-party system. However, an improved environment does not automatically translate into better discharge of functions, unless the obtaining political culture is favourable. It is to this other important dimension that we now turn, via examination of selected empirical survey data.

An empirical illustration of selected aspects of the MP's work environment

Support of major socio-political actors to MPs

One of the important aspects of the MP's work environment is the degree of support he/she gets from key social, political and economic actors at various levels. This analysis limits itself to the following actors: local government, central government, the party at constituency and national levels, voters and non-governmental organisations.

Following from the assumption that the amount of support the MP gets from local government will affect his/her performance as a representative, a sample of MPs were asked whether local government at constituency level facilitated or constrained their functions. The results unveil some interesting observations. A good 71.5 per cent of the interviewed MPs say that local government at constituency level gives them support of varying degrees and through various means. Those who say that local government does not help constitute the minority at 7.1 per cent and most of these are opposition MPs who account for 15.0 per cent of the sample. At the negative extreme, 14.3 per cent say that their local government constrains their work in a variety of ways. All of these belong to the opposition except for two CCM MPs. These opposition MPs attribute their constraints to local government's refusal to give them such work-related resources as money; denial of cooperation in planning and execution of constituency development; mobilising people against the MP and withholding important information. Those MPs who felt constrained in their duties by local government constitute a significant 40 per cent of all interviewed opposition MPs. It is interesting to note that no single CCM MP complained about being constrained in any of the ways mentioned above. The net picture emerging is that, to a great extent, MPs receive support from local government, but some opposition MPs who probably work with ruling party dominated councils are yet to enjoy such support.

A similar question was asked about whether central government facilities or constrains the MP's work. The overwhelming majority of MPs at 81.7 per cent acknowledged receiving some form of support from the central government. Some 10 per cent said the central government did not help and all of these but one were opposition MPs. It is interesting to note that not a single opposition MP acknowledged central government support in the following areas: receiving work-related resources; receiving co-operation in providing services to the constituency; encouraging people to heed the MP's advice; seeking the MP's advice on various issues and providing important information to the MP. In contrast, 37.3 per cent of the CCM MPs have acknowledged central government support in at least one of the above areas. It is thus apparent that the central government is even more supportive of the MPs than local government, but even here the relatively disadvantaged position of opposition MPs makes itself felt.

MPs were further asked to say whether or not their respective parties at constituency level supported them in their work. Only a tiny minority at 8.6 per cent gave no indication of such support, as against 91.4 per cent who expressed varying degrees of support. This is as encouraging as it is not surprising. However, it is interesting to note that whereas not a single opposition MP expressed lack of support from the party at constituency level, 12.5 per cent of CCM MPs did. This may be confirming what we said earlier about the emerging autonomy of MPs from the party, and the number involved is not negligible.

Nevertheless, such autonomy is not yet apparent with regard to opposition MPs, who as individuals, probably still lack enough political roots in the constituencies.

The party at national level is also highly acknowledged as a giver of support to MPs. The overwhelming majority of 98.5 per cent say they received some form of support from the party at national level. There is one CCM voice which does not acknowledge help even at national level, as against not a single opposition MP denying receiving such support. Here again, this suggests some burgeoning autonomy of the representative from the party, even at national level, unless we are dealing here with just an isolated case.

MPs also, by and large, enjoy the support of voters in their respective constituencies. Some 96.1 per cent admit receiving some support from the voters. Both ruling party and opposition MPs have indicated that the highest support they have received from the voters is in the form of work-related resources such as money (ruling party 18.5 per cent, opposition 22.7 per cent). This suggests that, in both camps, the voters have become significant providers, perhaps in such areas as financing campaigns. If this be the case, it confirms our earlier suggestion that MP candidates under multipartysm have reduced their dependence on the party in campaign financing and procurement of other resources. The findings also show that the one single area of support shared by all MPs, from both camps, is voter cooperation in developing the constituency.

As far as support from non-governmental organisations to MPs is concerned, 68.4 per cent of the MPs have said that NGOs help in their work, while 15.8 per cent said they do not help. Another 15.8 per cent gave other answers, which do not categorically acknowledge or deny the existence of NGO support. Overall, this shows that the majority of MPs are aware that they can at least potentially avail themselves of

NGO support. This is in line with the assertion we made earlier, and it is a positive development, which allows the enterprising MP to mobilise resources from this relatively new base.

From the foregoing, it can be concluded that, to a great extent, MPs currently enjoy support from local and central government, their respective political parties at both constituency and national levels, voters and non-governmental organisations. This is an important area in the environment which surrounds the work of MPs and it is favourable. In some of the discussed relationships, opposition MPs still experience constraints, particularly in matters of co-operation and material support. But this is hardly surprising, when it is viewed in the context of the novelty of multipartysm in the country.

The political culture environment

The prevalence of major actor support to MPs can go a long way to facilitating the latter's work, but it can do so only in combination with other favourable political culture factors. These include the MP's own conceptualisation of the importance of his/her work; the motivation behind seeking the office of MP; the real or perceived power and authority associated with being an MP; the level of understanding of the logic of democratic representation among the population (accountability, responsiveness, the locus of loyalty, etc). In this section, we examine the status of only two such factors and try to figure out whether or not they positively complement the favourable environment of major actor support to MPs. We will focus on the MP's motivation to seek office and the power and authority associated with being an MP.

With regard to why people contest for the office of MP, samples of MPs and voters were asked to explain why people contest to become MPs. The results are shown in Table 5.1 below.

Table 5.1: Why people contest to become MPs

S/N	Value label	Mp's responses		Voters' responses	
		Frequency	%	Frequency	%
1.	Remuneration package	26	26.0	185	29.0
2.	Opportunities	23	23.0	87	13.0
3.	Prestige	15	15.0	26	4.1
4.	Prospects for upward Mobility	1	1.0	8	1.3
5.	To serve constituency	23	23.0	120	18.8
6.	To serve the nation			69	10.8
7.	Other	4	4.0	13	2.0
8.	DK/NR	8	8.0	131	20.5
	Total	100	100.0	639	100.0

From the above findings, both MPs and voters single out remuneration package as the highest motivating factor behind seeking the office of MP at 26 per cent and 29 per cent, respectively. Disregarding the high DK/NR 20.5 per cent category among voter respondents, the next high motive is 'serving the constituency' which is exposed by 23 per cent of the MPs and 18.8 per cent of the voters. If one left the emerging big picture at this, one would be tempted to say that there is a healthy balance between personal gain and civic service as motivating factors. However, this apparent balance collapses when all the factors expressing individual benefit are added up. In the case of MPs, the individualistic motives account for 65 per cent of all the responses, while the same account for 47.4 per cent of the voters. This suggests that the pursuit of individual benefits is by far the greatest motive to seek the office of MP.

This being the case, it is clear that the work of the average MP will be dominated by the pursuit of individualistic interests, followed by some modest input in the service of the constituency. The functions relating to serving the national interest are not likely to be on the MP's agenda, and this is confirmed by the fact that none of the MPs said they were motivated by the urge to serve the nation. This may be a by-product of the proposition we made earlier, that under the current multipartyism, understanding of the notion of the country's 'national interest' is no longer obvious.

We can therefore conclude that this combination of a culture of possessive individualism and the apparently diminished value of 'national interest' do negatively affect the MP in fulfilling his/her broad representative duties as they have been outlined earlier in this chapter.

The second political culture factor that is likely to affect the MP's performance of his/her functions is the real or perceived power and authority associated with the representative. In this regard, MPs were asked to characterise the amount of power and authority representatives have at constituency and national levels. The results are shown in Table 5.2 below:

Table 5.2: MPs' power and authority at constituency and national levels

S/N	Responses on levels of power/authority									
	Very high level authority		Sufficient authority		Insufficient authority		No authority at all		Total	
	Frequency	%	Frequency	%	Frequency	%	Frequency	%	Frequency	%
1. Tanzania MP's authority at constituency level responsibilities	1	1.5	11	16.9	50	77.0	3	4.6	65	100.0
2. Tanzania MP's authority at national level responsibilities	2	3.1	16	25.0	43	67.2	3	4.7	64	100.0

The above results show that the majority of MPs perceive their level of power/authority to be insufficient both at constituency level (77.0 per cent) and at national level (67.2 per cent). This is not surprising, given the assembly-cabinet fusion, the powers of the executive and the party whip functions discussed earlier. Those who acknowledge that their power/authority is sufficient are much fewer (16.9 per cent at constituency level and 25.0 per cent at national level). It is interesting to note that the majority in this category of MPs feel they have more sufficient power/authority at national level than at constituency level. This finding seems to correlate with our earlier finding that MPs get more support from central government than local government at constituency level.

It is thus probable that this majority of MPs who feel they have insufficient power/authority both at national and constituency levels will tend to discharge their functions with caution or even timidity. Such a situation is likely to inhibit creativity and initiative and perhaps even elevate the already entrenched individualistic interests further above those of the nation and the constituents. The prevailing power/authority equation cannot but constrain the MP in his/her work, but this should not be an excuse for the MP not to exploit those recent gains in autonomy that we have associated with multipartyism. Some intelligent exploitation of those gains may make-up for certain deficits in power and authority.

To conclude this section, we learn that the two political culture values examined above do not enhance the quality of the environment in which the MP works. The overridingly individualistic motives that push people to contest the office of MP and the apparent lack of nationalism do not augur well for the good discharge of the MPs' representative functions, even in a situation where they get adequate support from the major actors. Similarly, the pervasive feeling among the majority of MPs that they do not have enough power/authority works counter to the MPs' self-actualisation in their roles, even in a situation where the multiparty environment has clearly enhanced their political leverage and latitude, especially *vis a vis* their parties and to some extent the presidency. These negative factors are likely to be exacerbated by other inadequacies in the country's civic culture, such as low citizen competence among the general public, which tends to make representatives more complacent if not outright negligent.

The financial, material and human resource factor

In the performance of their duties, MPs need adequate financial, material and human resources. In this area, many MPs have voiced complaints with regard to shortages or lack of such resources. For example, Makidara Mosi (2000: 131) has lamented the MPs' inability to increase political competence among their constituents, partly because of:

> ...their small financial capacity and lack of work tools. Many of the MPs' offices in the regions have no basic office equipment such as computers, typewriters, etc. (Free translation from Kiswahili).

This is by and large a correct statement. However, under current circumstances this need not be the case, provided the MP has learnt to tap into the decentralised resource base. Where the central government is unable to provide adequate funding, the enterprising MP can raise funds from NGOs, foreign donors, local businesses, and even the local government in the constituency. The solution to this problem should be found in the MP's going to work to mobilise resources and not in getting the resources from government so that the MP can go to work.

In our view, at present MPs are not justified to blame their non-performance of their duties on lack of transportation or bad remuneration. Some people used to argue that the government loans to MPs to purchase personal vehicles (the so-called *'shangingi'*) were not an adequate work incentive because MPs used much of their salaries to service the loan at the expense of the quality of their livelihood and their future financial security. This may have been the case then, which we doubt. But now, after the passing of legislation that gives them a gratuity of some twenty million shillings after completion of each parliamentary term, we are talking of an unprecedented financial incentive in their favour. Add this to a similar benefit after each subsequent term, then the motivation increases exponentially.

Thus, as far as the financial and material resources are concerned, the environment has satisfied the MPs' prime motive to pursue individual gains as depicted in Table 5.1 above. They now have no excuse not to perform well. After all, the better they perform, the better chance they stand to be re-elected and continue reaping the benefits after each term.

One lacking component in the MP's resource base is the human resource component in the form of staff or aides. In advanced countries, like the US or Britain, representatives have aides who give advice on policy, do research, organise civic functions, do fund-raising, lobby the local council, etc. These are services that our MPs do not have, and this is a serious omission in our view. This human resource facility ought to be made available to the MPs and of course this has budgetary implications that both central and local governments must address. One possible starting point could be the institution of internship programmes for tertiary level students in relevant fields at offices of MPs.

We thus conclude that MPs at present have a potentially good work environment as far as financial and material resources are concerned. Where these are inadequate because the government cannot fund certain activities, clever MPs can fend for themselves by forging ties with unorthodox providers, who can now be easily sought out and found. Providing MPs with a team of aides will make the environment even better. We need to add that efforts to improve the work environment of MPs should pay particular attention to the MPs for the special seats (47 after the 2000 general elections), who seem to enjoy less work facilities than their constituency counterparts.

Conclusion

In this chapter, we have attempted to assess the nature of the MP's work environment in Tanzania in successive historical settings. We have observed that this environment has changed. Under the one-party system, the environment was severely constrained as the MP functioned at the total mercy of the powerful single party and the executive branch of its government. The assembly-cabinet fusion, the supremacy of the single party, the much-feared party whip, the centralisation of political power and resources, all stood together as formidable fetters to the MP's autonomy particularly in the area of personal-level functions and in functions relating to personal convictions and conscience.

However, in functions relating to consideration of the 'national interest,' the environment was very favourable because unlike today, there was a well-defined and consensual understanding of what the country's 'national interest' was.

Under the current multiparty system, the MP's work environment has improved in some areas. For example, the parties' grip over their representatives has slightly loosened, although MPs still face the constraint of losing their seats once they cross the floor or get expelled from the party. However, an incumbent MP is now more likely to be re-nominated by his/her party more on the basis of his/her electability than on the basis of his/her standing on the patronage scale. In the worst of conditions, an MP can now seek re-election on the ticket of a different party. The MP can mobilise resources independently from the now diversified resource base. Thus, multipartyism has elevated the MP's relative autonomy, enabling him/her to better perform personal-level functions and constituency-level functions. But the performance of functions relating to considerations of the 'national interest' has become rather difficult, because the multiparty era has severely altered the once consensual understanding of the country's 'national interest'.

At another level, the current legal setting has given some relief to MPs vis a vis the executive branch of government. MPs have been granted the legal weapon of impeaching the president, and now the latter can only dissolve parliament under more stringent conditions. This also adds to an improved work environment for the MP.

Another index of the propiciousness of the MPs' current work environment is the high level of support they get from important actors such as the local and central governments, their parties, the voters and non-governmental organisations. The majority of MPs have acknowledged support of varying degrees from each of the above actors, and such support enriches the MP's work environment. However, there is a significant number of opposition MPs who claim that they either receive no help from the local and central governments, or that their work is actually constrained by these establishments. Of these two, local government at constituency level is more blamed. Even the current resource package available to MPs creates a reasonably good work environment, despite commonly made assertions to the contrary. Vehicles for mobility in the constituencies are provided on loan, the gratuity given after each term of office is generous, and the enterprising MP can mobilise other miscellaneous resources from various private and corporate sources with which he/she can forge ties at will. What the MP lacks is staff or aides, and this is an area that requires government action.

But all the above improvements in the MP's work environment cannot be put to maximum use unless the general area of civic competence in the country improves. The current situation suggests that civic competence is low in certain key areas. For example, it appears that by far the greatest motive to seek the office of MP is the pursuit of individual benefits that the office can generate. This dominant culture of possessive individualism diminishes the important values of nationalism and civic duty, and it may be a deadly recipe for mercenary, instead of popular representation. Secondly, the majority of MPs perceive their level of power and authority to be insufficient both at constituency and national levels. This perception, real or imagined, may inhibit the MPs' creativity and initiative in their work. Under the pretext of powerlessness, they may discharge their functions with undue caution or timidity, or even unjustifiable negligence. Much remains to be done in the general civic culture environment to further improve the quality of the MP's work environment.

References

Friedrich, C, (1968). *Constitutional Government and Democracy: Theory and Practice in Europe and America,* 4th edition, Waltham, Massachussets: Blaidsdell Publishing Company.

Makidara, M, (2000). *"Namna ya Kujenga Uwezo wa Kisiasa wa Raia: Mtazamo wa Mbunge Wa Upinzani",* in Rwekaza S. Mukandala and Joshua S. Madumula (eds.), *"Ujenzi wa Uwezo wa Kisiasa wa Mtanzania",* Dar es Salaam REDET.

Msekwa, P. (1995), *Essays on the Transition to Multi-Partyism in Tanzania.* Dar es Salaam: DUP.

Nyalali Report (1991). *The Presidential Commission on Single Party or Multiparty System in Tanzania: Report and Recommendations of the Commission on the Democratic System in Tanzania.* Dar es Salaam.

Shivji, I.G., (1996). 'The G-55 Motion', in Kivutha Kibwana, *et al* (eds), *In Search of Freedom and Prosperity: Constitutional Reform in East Africa,* Nairobi: Claripress Ltd.

The United Republic of Tanzania (1990 Version), *The Constitution of the United Republic of Tanzania, 1977.* Dar es Salaam: Government Printer.

6

The Role of Members of Parliament as Representatives of the People

Athumani Liviga

Introduction

Mushi (this volume) has stated five essential principles of representation in a liberal democratic system, which Tanzania has opted to follow. These are that:
- The ultimate power lies with the people (the popular sovereignty principle);
- This popular power is exercised by a selected few on behalf of the many (the deputation principle);
- These deputies/representatives are mandated by the people through periodic elections (the popular consent principle);
- Decisions made and actions carried out by these deputies have a binding effect on the community (the governance principle); and
- As ultimate masters, the people remain the final judge of performance of the government and their deputies (the accountability principle).

These principles do, however, raise some basic theoretical as well as practical issues on questions of representation. The main debate has historically focused on whether the deputy or a member of parliament (MP) should be a delegate bound by an imperative mandate or one with a general, flexible mandate in which he can exercise discretion as a rational human being. While Rousseau favoured a representative bound by a rigid mandate, Burke (1901), on the other hand, argued for a representative with discretionary authority and guided by four main factors, namely:
- constituency views and opinions;
- rational judgements;

- national interests and
- representatives convictions and conscience.

Accordingly, as Moshi has pointed out (in this volume) that a functional analysis of these factors would lead to three basic functions performed by an MP in conformity with the Burkean ideal of representation. The functions are those:
- Based on views, opinions and interests of the constituents;
- Originating from the representative's own judgment of the situation as well as personal conviction and conscience; and
- Based on consideration of national interests.

In modern times, when politics of representation are discussed and practiced in most democracies, people tend to view and mould a representative in Burkean terms, i.e., a person with discretion and one who is inclined or expected to act in response to local, national and personal exigencies in fulfilling his/her role.

This chapter is concerned itself with dimension of democratic norms and processes in modern states namely, political representation. It seeks to understand the role of MPs in Tanzania by studying and analysing responses of interviewees who included both the voters and MPs themselves. In a nationwide survey on democratic norms and practices conducted in early 1999, the main questions asked were intended to seek information on two main areas relating to and concerning the role of MPs as representatives of the people.

In the first place, respondents were asked to enumerate factors which, in their opinion, attract people to contest in elections. Some of the factors included: MP remuneration package, opportunities, prospects, dignity, prestige, anticipation, service to constituents, and service to the nation.

Secondly, the respondents were required to show the extent to which parliamentarians adhere to their role of representation. In other words, to what extent do MPs follow the requirements and needs of the people they represent in conducting their activities; carrying out their functions; fulfilling their obligations and making their decisions within and outside parliamentary sessions? In this regard, the basic issues of concern were: the possibility of the people to have final say; the source of MPs' right to represent; whether or not the MPs are the basis of new policy/law; the effect of MPs supporting an unwanted policy; things done by MPs to impress the people; what makes voters elect a person; whether the voters know the names or their MPs; whether the MPs' gender effects the voters' choice and opinions on women's special seats programme.

The rest of this chapter is divided into three main parts. The first part addresses and analyses issues motivating people to contest parliamentary seats. The responses given by interviewees on whether material and non-material gains do motivate people to become MPs are then discussed. The major concern is to determine the extent to which these expected gains explain the desire of the aspirants to contest for membership of parliament. An analysis of whether or not people engage in parliamentary elections for specific gains is important because political representation demands that MPs should be totally committed to the affairs of the people within their constituencies. MPs should not be wavering in their activities and obligations or swaying and wanting within their functions and decisions due to interests other that those of the people they represent.

The second part documents, discusses and illustrates how MPs adhere to representation principles in adjudicating their functions, obligations, activities and decisions. The relationship between MPs and their constituencies is also analysed so as to determine whether or not the people being represented have the final say or who actually gives the MPs the right to represent and who are they responsible to, i.e., are the MPs accountable? If so to whom? The main interest is to see how, to what extent and by what means MPs fulfill their roles of representing the people.

It is also of interest to note the interplay of constituency and national interests that influences the functions of the MPs. An attempt is also made to show whether or not MPs are responsible for new policy/law and what things they do to impress the people being represented. Gender relationships are observed in order to understand the effect they have on parliamentary elections, political representation and opinion on women special seats programme. Gender mainstreaming in all aspects of life, including political life, is an important consideration within the fight for basic human and democratic rights all over the world. Such an understanding and practice by both voters and MPs demonstrate the extent to which Tanzanians in general value personal attributes and ability for performance rather than gender differences in electing their MPs.

The last part summarises some of the salient features in determining MPs' role as representatives. This includes aspirations to become parliamentarians, ability to adhere to representation roles and the consequences of the interplay between the MPs in representing the people. The confluence of these various interests, which at times may conflict with one another, could explain the extent to which MPs adhere to representation.

As Burke noted, parliament should not be seen as congress of ambassadors representing different and hostile interests but should rather be regarded as a unified assembly of one nation, with one major interest, that of the whole; where neither local purposes nor local prejudices ought to guide, but for the general good. While to deliver an opinion is the right of all men; that of constituents is a weighty and respectable opinion which a representative ought always to rejoice to hear and which he always ought to consider most seriously (Burke, 1901). It is within this context that the representative's unbiased opinion, mature judgment and enlightened conscience, derived neither from the constituency nor from the law and constitution but from providence, should be practiced and maintained in undertaking the role of representation.

Factors motivating people to become members of parliament

Parliamentary seats are hotly contested in Tanzania. Elections are also held for a purpose: to get people's representatives to make collective and interest decisions on behalf of the people being represented. Elections therefore perform several important political functions, including facilitating peaceful change of leadership and representing the general population in the decision-making bodies of government. They also provide the basis for the legitimacy of the government through the collective mandate voluntarily given by the electorate to the leadership. Elections, when free and fair, help to uphold the rule of law, promote and safeguard democracy by reminding the leadership that it obtains authority from the people and that it has to be responsible and accountable for its actions (Liviga, 1999). Yet, such a situation can only be attained if both the electorate and those elected do understand the roles of MPs as representatives of their constituencies and the nation where personal, constituency and national interests may not always be acting in conformity or complementarity (Liviga, 1999).

However, under the multiparty system in Tanzania and even one-party state, the competition among aspirants has always been tough, sometimes rough and often unfair as exemplified by numerous appeals within party hierarchies and through the judicial machinery. This indicates that these positions have certain gains, which make contestants compete vigorously within party caucuses and during constituency elections. However, it would be difficult, if these positions had no privileges, to attract people, especially when the role of representatives becomes a full time job. The representative is also required to champion the constituency interests in the National Assembly where laws are enacted that affect such interests in one way or the other. The MPs work of looking for information and data, influencing institutions and organs and debating, discussing and voting to pass laws is time consuming and knowledge demanding. It needs equally appropriate remuneration to attract committed and competent people to fulfill the tasks.

In order to explain why people want to become MPs, a number of questions were asked to both voters and MPs themselves. The questions aimed at establishing factors attracting people to contest parliamentary elections and ultimately become MPs. One of the questions asked the voters to enumerate the reasons for politicians' contest for parliamentary seats.

Generally it can be said that Tanzanian voters believe that remuneration is the most important reason attracting people to aspire for parliamentary seats. Yet others think that desire to serve the constituency and the nation is equally important. However, compared to remuneration (29 per cent) serving constituency (18.8 per cent) and serving the nation (10.8 per cent) appear to be marginal. A combination of remuneration, opportunities and prestige (46.6 per cent) is more attractive than serving constituency and the nation (29.6 per cent). Nonetheless, a substantial number of Tanzanians (20.5 per cent) did not indicate why politicians want to become MPs. This may either due to the fact some Tanzanians do not follow political affairs or generally fear to state their positions publicly.

However, even when the remuneration package is removed from the variables attracting politicians to become MPs prestige and opportunities for personal gains still seem to be more important (22.9 per cent) than the urge to give service to constituencies and the nation combined (20.9 per cent). In this case more than half (51.6 per cent) of the people did not know what really attracts contestants, outside the sphere of material gains or other incentives, to become MPs.

When both remuneration and opportunities were not considered as factors, percentages of expression did not change much in favour of other variables being considered. In this case service to constituencies takes a slight lead of 7.5 per cent over prestige which stands at 5.8 per cent, relatively above service to the nation at 5.6 per cent. The combined effect of service to constituencies and the nation is only 13.1 per cent compared to remuneration package alone which stands at 29 per cent taking the lead on the motivating factors for people to assume MPs roles. But the number of people who either didn't know or didn't want to make their opinion known shot up to 71.5 per cent. This would seem to indicate that once you remove material and non-material gains as motivating factors, most voters (71.5 per cent) did not know what other factors motivated politicians to become MPs. It would also seem that the high percentage (71.5 per cent) of uncertainty strongly indicates that while service to constituencies and to the nation are important factors, they are not the leading ones. This picture becomes much clearer when one looks at the constituencies that participated in the interviews to see what the expressions were. Out of the twelve, Bukene and Mbeya Urban voted well above fifty per cent (75 and 57.5 per cent respectively) to indicate that people were attracted by remuneration packages in becoming MPs. These two were closely followed by Nkenge (41 per cent) service to the constituencies and the nation did not come out strongly as the national score was only 18.8 per cent and 10.8 per cent respectively. In Moshi Rural and Nkenga 37.5 per cent and 33.3 per cent of the voters respective said that service to constituency was an important attribute, while in Vunjo 42.5 per cent of the voters said that service to the nation is an important factor for people aspiring to become MPs. It is interesting to note that Mbeya

Urban and Bukene are high-density areas where industrial development and employment issues are emerging as critical aspects of modern life. Moshi Rural and Vunjo, on the other hand, are agricultural areas, which once had strong MPs who assisted the constituencies to get, for example, markets for coffee. These results indicate that Tanzanians in general believe that personal, material and non-material gains rather than service attract people who contest parliamentary elections. The voters clearly showed that people want to become MPs in order to acquire wealth and boost their income through MP remuneration packages and other opportunities which come with these positions.

When MPs themselves were asked to mention their sources of income they came up with MP remuneration (49 per cent), farming (22 per cent) and business/trading (11 per cent) as the only three viable indicators for the question. Almost half (49 per cent) of all MPs indicated that their income/wealth comes mainly by virtue of being MPs. These positions give them far more income than their farming and business/trading activities combined (33 per cent). Their admission also suggests that for those who are not engaged in farming and business/trading activities, MPs remuneration packages are the only source of income. In fact, in the past, and especially under one-party rule, MPs were not allowed to engage in any commercial activities or even hold leadership positions in business undertakings. Hence, MP remuneration packages are, indeed, the most important reason for people to want to become MPs as voters pointed out and the MPs themselves agreed.

MPs were further requested to give reasons for contesting parliamentary elections. The results also confirmed the above scenario. More than half of all the MPs (64 per cent) admitted that material and non-material gains, such as remuneration packages, opportunities and dignity, attracted them the most to contest parliamentary elections. In this category MPs remuneration packages became the single leading factor (26 per cent) in attracting people to contest. The MPs consented that service to their constituencies took a second place and tallies with their desire to seek opportunities, which stood at 23 per cent. But without including remuneration package, the service category, i.e. combining service to constituencies and the nation makes them a leading reason for contesting by 44 per cent. Similarly, 25 per cent of all MPs indicate that service to constituencies is the most compelling factor for contesting elections after the remuneration packages.

Two issues emerge namely: even when remuneration package was removed from the gains category, the other three elements (opportunities, dignity and prospects) were still considered as strong reasons for contesting with 29 per cent. Secondly, the number of MPs who either did not know or did not want to make their own ideas known to the public increased from 8 per cent to 14 per cent. This is perhaps an indication that once remuneration packages are removed from the group of factors attracting people to contest, then even MPs themselves would not know what else could attract them most.

Where remuneration packages and opportunities were not considered as factors attracting competitors, the service category led by 38 per cent although it was still below 44 per cent. Service to the nation at 25 per cent became more important than service to constituency at 13 per cent. The gains category also dropped from 29 per cent to 19 per cent. Moreover, the number of MPs who declared that there were still other factors that account for their contesting elections has risen from 3 per cent to 9 per cent. The percentage of those who either didn't know or who could not reveal why they go for parliamentary positions has also increased to 34 per cent. This further confirms that material gains are the leading motivating factor for people to contest the elections.

In a multiparty electoral setting this general picture needs to be further examined from another angle taking into account party affiliations, allegiances and commitments. In this light, the responses from MPs were looked at to see what attracted them most to contest, as members of their respective political parties. In analysing the situation CCM formed the ruling party category while the rest of the parties constitute opposition party category. According to these responses, both ruling party and opposition MPs said, remuneration packages, in terms of salaries and opportunities, are important reasons for contesting parliamentary seats. While more than half opposition MPs (54 per cent) mentioned these reasons as the most important, only 47.1 per cent of their counterparts from the ruling party voiced the same reason. However, MPs from the opposition seemed also to be motivated by service to the constituencies (31 per cent) whereas only

18 per cent from the ruling party said so. Dignity ranked higher for MPs from the ruling party than the opposition at 20 per cent and 3.4 per cent respectively. This should not be surprising since under one-party rule, people from the same party were contesting all the constituencies. MPs from the ruling party seemed therefore to be defending their positions and losing a seat is interpreted as losing face or dignity.

Another interesting divide is that between Tanzania mainland and Zanzibar. The responses from these two parts beat the party affiliation split shown above to keep the geographical and economic level imperatives and differences. While 45.5 per cent of the MPs from Zanzibar are strongly led to contest by service to their constituencies, their counterparts from the mainland are led by remuneration packages and opportunities (53.8 per cent) followed by personal dignity at 16.7 per cent. To the MPs fro Zanzibar remuneration and opportunities together constitute 31 per cent while dignity is only 9.1 per cent.

The MPs responses shade light on why elections are vehemently contested within party caucuses and at the open constituency level. There is no doubt therefore that those who aspire for these elections see an MP's position as a source of income. The MP remuneration packages and other opportunities related to MP positions are quite lucrative. According to the constitution only the MPs can be chosen to become ministers. Ministerial posts carry with them good salaries and attractive remuneration packages, prestige and dignity. All these aspects lead to other socio-economic opportunities for themselves, their families, friends, close relatives and associates, both within and outside the country.

Other incentives for MPs include becoming board members, which in Tanzania, is lucrative in terms of remuneration and other fringe benefit. It is mostly the MPs who are chosen to lead and become members of various commissions formed either by the president, cabinet ministers or parliament itself. Commission members are normally paid a lot of money and other benefits for a short duration. Furthermore, MPs positions attract a handsome gratuity at the end of every five years. Given the high remuneration packages, the pension schemes for retired MPs are also very attractive. An MP's position is the only government employment category or cadre, which is not limited by age. It therefore attracts even retired officials from the public service cadre, the armed forces and others to contest, earning more money after retiring from their various professional service categories. This is on top of their accessibility to government loans and other institutions including banks and funds, a factor that explains the fierce contests.

MPs' adherence to representation and their relationship with constituencies

This section shows the extent to which MPs adhere to their role of representing their constituencies. Adherence to representational role will depend, among other things, on how MPs take into account the needs and wishes of the people while deliberating, discussing and deciding upon various matters of interest to the stakeholders from their constituencies. This is done to determine the extent to which the voters' interests are integrated into the work of their parliamentarians. The issue is to find out whether or not the voters are consulted before and/ or during the parliamentary sessions which deliberate upon, and take various decisions on matters affecting their lives.

The loyalty and accountability of representatives should naturally go to the voters in line with the principle of popular sovereignty. But within the Tanzanian parliamentary system this principle is compromised under the National Assembly/executive fusion because there is relatively strong government control. Moreover, the introduction of mass politics has created organised and disciplined mass party's task of mass mobilisation and membership recruitment on a national scale. This situation leads to the bureaucratisation of politics whereby emphasis is put on the party and 'party government'. In such a system the executive president can dissolve parliament; while the political parties have strong party whips to induce members to toe 'party line'. The whip undermines the retaliatory weapons of the representative i.e. the 'power of the purse' and 'motion of no confidence.'

Thus, the loyalty and accountability of representatives are usually shared among the voters, the party and party government. Generally, it is the party rather than the voters who can hold the MPs accountable in between elections. The MPs, on the other hand, cannot rely on their own conscience. They need to abide by party decisions where, as party cadres, they have to accept, propagate, and support the constitution and the election manifestos of their parties during elections.

On whether the people have the final say on the roles of the MPs in the National Assembly, more than 66 per cent of the people mentioned the voters as having the final say while only 7 per cent rejected the idea. Those who mentioned other elements that have the final say constituted 26.3 per cent. The leading constituencies in this regard were Arusha Urban (42 per cent), Vunjo (37.5 per cent), Bukoba Rural (37.5 per cent) and Nzega East (35 percewnt). These results indicate that there is no significant discrepancy between the perceptions of the people in rural and urban districts over this issue. It also becomes clear that there are no big variations in the figures, which are all below 50 per cent. However, other constituencies (44.4 per cent) emphatically expressed the view that the question of controlling MPs will depend on the operating environment. The leading constituencies are Mbeya Urban and Mtwara Rural which both stand at 53.8 per cent, followed by Bukoba Rural (52 per cent) and Bukene at 50 per cent.

When the MPs were asked whether the people should have the final say on activities of MPs, 49.1 per cent replied that this would depend on, among other things, the people's voting capacity, the taxes that they pay, the need to promote democracy and people's knowledge of their civic and other rights. Only 26.3 per cent of he MPs thought that there are other entities, which have the final say. When expressing their own opinions as party members, the MPs answers were geared towards group presentation and party adherence to the ruling and opposition party lines. The MPs were basically in agreement (37.7 per cent and 37.9 per cent) with the proposition that there are entities, other than the people, which have the final say over their roles. MPs from the ruling party further stated that the voters have the final say and they can make choices (15.9 per cent). The opposition MPs maintained that though this reason is important (10.3 per cent) taxpayers should have the right to have a final say (10.3 per cent). This was in contrast with their counterparts from the ruling party who seemed not to value this aspect (1.4 per cent)

On the question of who gives the MPs the right to represent, the responses show that there are mainly two sources, i.e. the voters and the constitution/law, 62.3 per cent of the voters said it is them who give the MPs the right to represent. Other variables such as the constitution/law, parties and the government were ranked low (5.9 per cent, 7.4 per cent and 9.1 per cent) respectively. The MPs, on the other hand, differed with the voters and constitution/law attributed the right to represent to the constitution/law (78 per cent). Only 22 per cent mentioned voters as determinants of MPs right to represent.

When certain variables are removed as possible sources of the MP's right to represent, the pattern changes. For example, when the constitution/law is removed as a source of the MPs' right to represent, the percentage of voters as a source rises from 62.3 per cent to 87.3 per cent. All constituencies except one, mentioned voters as a source at 50 per cent and above. As for MPs, when the constitution/law is removed from the list of possible sources, voters became a major source (73 per cent). Furthermore, when education is factored in for the MPs their position as regards the source of their right to represent remains the constitution/law. The source was 100 per cent for those with primary education, 82.4 per cent for secondary school leavers 77.8 per cent for higher learning institutions and 75.9 per cent for graduates, giving an average of 78 per cent. The average for MPs on voters as a source with respect to the same education categories was 21 per cent.

The crucial fact here is that both the voters and the MPs cite different but extremely interdependent sources of political representation. It can be argued that voters are to see the MPs as their deputies chosen through elections to represent them in parliament. The direct representation system practiced by the small Greek city states, is ruled out by the sheer size of the country. The voters therefore rightly consider those that MPs are democratically elected representatives of the people whose tenure logically ceases as soon as the people withdraw their representative power, authority and legitimacy through elections. Voters exercised their democratic right to choose their representatives after every five years according to the requirements of the constitution, which is the fundamental/basic law of the country. That is why the MPs believe that the constitution/law is the source of their right to represent the people. Had it not been provided for in the constitution, neither would the voters be able to elect their MPs nor would the MPs stand for parliamentary elections.

The responses show that both groups agree that the voters and the constitution/law are important in giving the MPs their legitimacy as representatives of the people. But there is a big gap in terms of understanding the basic source of the MPs' right to the people related to their functions and obligations. For if the MPs don't derive their right to represent from the voters it would be difficult for them to champion the interests of, and be responsible to, these voters on a continuous basis. This partly explains why some MPs do not necessarily live in their constituencies, or visit them on a regular basis except at election time. It is equally not easy to envisage the MPs or even the National Assembly for that matter, cherishing the interests of the voters, if the MPs' right of representation is not derived from the electorate. After all the Constitution does not provide for MPs' accountability to their constituents. They can only take their MPs to task when the latter express the intention of seeking re-election.

But it is equally illogical to understand the voter's rights outside constitutional stipulations and provisions. The problem is that the constitution in Tanzania is not a popular product of the people, discussed by all in either a Constitutional Conference or Constituent Assembly. The constitution is therefore not well understood and often overwhelms and confuses the people over their rights. The relationship between the MPs and the constitution needs to be understood. The constitution should advance, emphasize and promote the interests of all the people within the country. All social groups could agree upon its underlying principles and provisions give it popular legitimacy rather than merely the legal character, in order to avoid political confusion and conflicting constitutional interpretations.

The role and functions of the MPs have immense implications on other arms of government, as well as on independent institutions, civil organisations, the private sector and the general public. As the highest law making body in the country, the decisions of parliament are legally binding to all people, once they become law. In this sense the people become interested and sometimes keen in following parliamentary deliberations to see the extent to which MPs articulate voters' interests.

On the question of the MPs' accountability for their actions, opinions and judgements, respondents said MPs were responsible to their constituents - 51.2 per cent of voters pointed out that the MPs are responsible to the voters rather than the party (17 per cent) the government (16.7 per cent), 55.6 per cent of the MPs replied that they were responsible to the voters and not to the government (13 per cent).

When both the people and MPs were requested to give their opinion on what is the basis for new policies, the two groups agreed that the constituency needs are basically the source for any new policy/law. The people through their vote confirmed this by 56 per cent although a good number of them (26 per cent) were not sure what exactly constituted the basis for any new policy/law. With respect to constituencies over 60 per cent maintained that constituency needs were the basis for any new policy/law while the remainder polled below 50 per cent. It is not surprising that voters tend to emphasise this fact because MPs are elected to basically represent the people. What the voters' responses seem to indicate is that national interests should be understood from the point of view and interests of the constituencies, which are not always held high when considering national needs and requirements.

The MPs would consider national interest (41 per cent) to be the source of new policy/law if constituency interests are not included among the sources. When party opinions and national interests were regarded as sources, leaving out constituency interests, party opinions became an important source (42 per cent) compared to national interests (31 per cent). This is contrary to the views expressed by voters whose score for party views, excluding national and constituency interests, were extremely low (4.1 per cent) The vast majority of voters (90.5 per cent) do not know what else should be the source of the new policy/law passed in parliament. Even when some factors are not considered, the responses still confirm the voter's position in relation to sources of new policy/law.

This dichotomy is a function of the party whip system in the National Assembly, which demands that MPs follow their party lines with regard to debates and decisions, playing one party against the other. Hence, party views and opinions become variables to be considered by MPs from both the ruling and opposition parties when discussing and voting for or against a new policy/law. It is perhaps this strict adherence to party politics, affiliations and conflict, among others, which sometimes force MPs to support policies contrary to the voters interests. Asked what would be their response to such a situation most voters opted 'reject the MPs' (70.1 per cent) against 17.8 per cent who said such MPs could still be accepted. The voters who said MPs acceptance or rejection should depend on the circumstances under which their decisions were made were insignificant (5.55 per cent).

When MPs were asked whether it was justified to support policies or laws that their constituents did not want, 43.1 per cent felt that it all depends on the kind of policy under consideration and the type of interests which are jeopardised by such a policy. Other MPs (23.1 per cent) felt that voters have no right to go against decisions of their MPs. The rest of the MPs felt that people should have been consulted prior to supporting the policy and, if not, the voters reserved disagree with their representatives (25.1 per cent)

From the above discussion it is clear that while the people say they have a right to reject MPs who go against their interests and wishes, the MPs maintain that the voters do not have such a right. The MPs seem to say that voters should try to understand the circumstances under which the decisions were made by their MPs, because such parliamentary decisions are often dictated by the prevailing environment. In other words, in taking parliamentary decisions, factors and interests other than those of constituencies come into play and often take the upper hand. The dichotomy is very fundamental to the question of political representation as it shows whether MPs are to rigidly abide by the dictates of their constituencies or should use their rational judgment in making decisions. Nevertheless, even those constituencies, which voted heavily in favour of rejecting MPs who support unwanted policies, cannot do so as there is no provision in the constitution for power of recall in between elections.

The gender of an MP as it affects compliance to and performance of parliamentary functions was one of the questions posed to the people and the MPs. The responses to this question were in favour of both sexes indicating that the gender divide was immaterial to political representation (62.5 per cent). The voters did not see why they should discriminate against any particular gender since the ability to perform would depend mainly on the individual's merit and was not necessarily determined by gender. In their experiences, other things being equal, both men and women performed equally. The fact is that all the people irrespective of their gender are electing every MP. The voters normally consider one's performance and outlook regardless of the gender divide.

While 67 per cent of the voters knew the names of their MPs, 58.6 per cent could not exactly remember the good things done that their MPs had done. On the other hand, 50 per cent of the MPs seem to remember up to five good things which they did, or gave, to impress their voters or constituencies. Although voters could not remember the good things done by MPs, 46.3 per cent mentioned that their choice for particular persons was influenced by competing parties against 42.3 per cent who mentioned the candidates themselves. Here it is worth noting, albeit in passing, that spending by either the candidates themselves or their respective parties was not an important factor in winning or losing the elections. This contradicts what happens in most post-election appeals which tend to stress corruption and rigging, implying that money or other material benefits were changing hands to buy favours from voters or those who could influence the result in favour of one candidate against the others.

Conclusion

This chapter studied political representation by looking at the role of MPs as representatives of the people in a survey conducted in early 1999. The questions were basically set to explore two fundamental factors; why people want to be MPs and how MPs adhere to representation. The summary of the theoretical underpinnings to the issues which constitute political representation and how it has been practiced throughout social history has been brought into play as a necessary background to the discussion. It also conducted the discussion within the political context and perspectives of the democratic norms and processes being introduced in Tanzania.

The study has shown that on the whole people would want to contest parliamentary seats in order to gain material and non-material benefits related to MPs' positions. The incomes of most MPs have been raised and some have prospered by virtue of their being MPs. Ministerial posts, board and commission membership and access to government loans and other fringe benefits, leading to dignity, opportunity, security, prestige and integrity / are some of the opportunities closely connected with parliamentary membership. Parliamentary elections in Tanzania have always been associated with intense competition, and sometimes unfair play and undue influence (corruption) have become the main claims in appeals filed in courts of law by losing candidates.

This study further shows that the people through their votes consider themselves as having the final say over their MPs. However, this situation is yet to be seen from any part of the country either within the constituencies or at the national level. The MPs, on the other, hand have claimed that their right to represent does not come from the electorate but rather stems from the constitution. This contradicts the view of the people who feel it is their votes that give the MPs the right to represent. The voters are of the opinion that it is they who deserve and reserve the right to reject all those MPs who support unwanted policy/law, an opinion that is not quite agreeable to the MPs.

There is a divergence of opinions regarding the relationship between the constitution, the people and the role of the MPs. For, while it stands to reason to consider the constitution as the source of representation, it is illogical to ignore the people . The constitution cannot exist without endorsement by the people either directly through a referendum or by their representatives in a constitutional conference or a constituent assembly. The constitution as it is now is not readily identifiable with the people nor does it give the power of recall to the voters. This state of affairs underplays the role of the people and gives MPs the pretext not to adequare adhering to their representative role. This is so even when MPs are in agreement with the people constituency interests should be the basis for new policy/law that is discussed and/or passed by parliament.

The gender divide according to the responses does not pose a serious problem during parliamentary elections. Candidates are elected according to their personal/party capacity, ability and other attributes to perform parliamentary functions. There is even agreement by the people that the special women seats programme and proportion should be enlarged. Voters have also shown that candidates are elected more on party lines and popularity of individual competitors rather than financial clout and other material wealth of candidates. This revelation poses a serious threat to political representation as it denies the existence, use and involvement of incentives and rigging to affect election results at both party caucuses and general election levels, which in turn compromises the rights and power of voters to influence public policy. Numerous post-election law suits suggest that parliamentary elections are not free of corrupt practices and indeed in some cases plaintiffs have presented sufficient evidence to nullify the election of winning candidates.

The findings show that in Tanzania people contest parliamentary elections basically for financial gains rather than for providing leadership and serving the people. Such individuals cannot take to heart the needs and demands of their people, or give priority to national development requirements. The MPs' assertion that their right to represent stems from the constitution is unfortunate. The voters, however, know that although the constitution is the basis law of the land sovereignty rests with the people. It is encouraging that the people are ready and willing to recall MPs who fail to conduct themselves in a manner that is compatible with parliamentary functions and obligations.

Tanzania has adopted and practices the Burkean definition of a representative with increasing emphasis on two of the three functions of a representative namely: carrying out functions or activities and taking decisions based on the representative's own judgment of the situation, personal conviction and conscience and carrying out functions or taking decisions based on consideration of national interests. But carrying out functions or fulfilling obligations based on the views, opinions and interests of the constituencies is receiving less and less attention. This is unfortunately exemplified by the fact that MPs hardly stay in, or visit, their constituencies regularly (modern communications technology notwithstanding), except during election campaigns. It is also exemplified by the MPs willingness to support unwanted policies/laws contrary to the interests of the people.

In view of the findings, it is proposed is that voters should be given powers to control their members of parliament who do not deliver as expected (power of recall). In specific terms, voters should be empowered to fire their MPs without waiting for the five-year term to elapse. Modalities to effect such control may be worked out between the electoral authorities, political parties and the National Assembly. Political parties on their own can also work out procedures to control their MPs who do not perform the roles they were elected for. These steps should also be enshrined in the constitution, compelling MPs not only to be closer to their constituents whose views, demands, needs and interests should always be taken into parliamentary deliberations.

Also Deliberate efforts must be made to educate voters and the general population on civic rights and obligations. A systematic effort needs to be made to ensure that people are capable of identifying self-serving candidates who aspire to membership of parliament for personal enrichment, and desisting from voting for candidates who use unconventional means to attain their goals. Changes to the electoral laws should also be effected to ensure voters (or would be voters) are given an opportunity to present objections to candidates that do not have the required qualifications. The procedure should be made simple and transparent in its implementation.

References

Biene, H, (1974). *Kenya: The Politics of Participation and Control*, Michigan University Press.

Burke, E. (1901). *Writings and Speeches*, Vol. II, Boston

Cliffe, L. (1967). *One Party Democracy: The 1965 Tanzania General Elections*, Nairobi: East African Publishing House.

Eckstein, H. and David Apter (eds.) (1963). *Comparative Politics: A Reader*, New York: The Free Press.

Fredrich, C.J. (1968). *Constitutional Government and Democracy: Theory and Practice in Europe and America*, Waltham, Massachusetts: Blaisdell Publishing Company.

Liviga, A.J. (1999). *"Framework Paper for Studying the Neighbourhood and Village Council Elections"*, unpublished REDET paper, Dar es Salaam.

Locke, J. (1690). *Two Treatises on Government*, London

Mayhew, D. (1987). Congress: The Electoral Connection in P. Woll, *American Government: Readings and Cases*, Boston: Little Brown and Company.

Mill, J.S. (1859). *"On Liberty, Utilitarianism and the Proper Functioning of Representative,"* in Eckstein and Apter (eds).

Mushi, S.S., R. Mukandala and M. Baregu (eds) (1998), *Tanzania's Political Culture: A Baseline Survey*, Dar es Salaam.

Saul, J. (1974). *Socialism and Participation: Tanzania's 1970 National Elections,* Dar es Salaam: Tanzania Publishing House.

Woll, P. (1987). *American Government: Readings and Cases*, Boston: Little Brown and Company.

Van Donge, J. K and Liviga, A. (1990). *"The 1985 Parliamentary Elections: a conservative election"*. In Othman, H. Bavu, I and Okema, M. (eds) *Tanzania: Democracy in Transition*, Dar es Salaam: Dar es Salaam University Press.

7

The Relationship of Members of Parliament with other Political Actors: Government, Own Party and Voters

Ernest T. Mallya

Introduction

This chapter looks at the relationship between members of parliament (MPs) as representatives of the people and three other actors – the government at both local and central levels, the political party to which the MP belongs and the voters in the constituency. The data was collected in a survey of a hundred MPs from both Tanzania mainland and Zanzibar and from all opposition parties in the 1995-2000 parliament. Firstly, the chapter looks at the precursors of the liberal democratic theory, which has the representative government as one of its key pillars. Secondly it looks at the meaning and origins of representative government and how MPs should relate to parties, voters and governments. The chapter then concludes by noting that representation in the developing world, just as it is in the developed world, is nowhere near perfect and in fact, it is more defective than it is in the developed world.

Tanzania's experience across time will be emphasised starting from the 1962-1992 period when only one political party was allowed in the system and the period after 1992 when a multiparty system was introduced. Between 1965 and 1992, the party was very powerful and controlled almost all political activities in the country. In fact, the constitution provided that all political activities should be done under the auspices of the party. The survey data collected during the current period of multipartyism is then be analysed to show the kind of relationship that exists between MPs and the actors mentioned above.

The precursors of the liberal democratic theory

Normative political theory and philosophy provide us with what should be the proper forms of political organisation in state setting, including the notion of representative government. These focus on what is desirable – what ought to be or what should be. The political writings of Locke and Mill to a large extent fall under this categorisation. These political thinkers contributed a lot to the transition from the absolutist to the liberal state in Europe. They tried to define the boundaries of the state authority as against the freedom of the civil society – the individual, the family and to some extent business life. Liberalism, therefore, came to be associated with a range of freedoms in matters of daily life. Liberalism was related to 'free and equal' individuals who had natural rights as human beings. The means to safeguard these rights, while at the same time regulating individual behaviour in the state context, was through a constitutional state, private property and the competitive market economy. Political affairs, therefore, became part of these freedoms, as will be explained further in the subsequent sections of this paper.

Thomas Hobbes (1588-1679) was among the first political thinkers to grapple with the question of the necessity of the state in organising human beings. He was of the opinion that the state (Leviathan) was necessary as an instance where sovereign authority should reside in order to avoid chaos that can emanate from human nature (Plamenatz, 1963),

In his postulations he came up with some elements of what was to be known as liberalism. These included the concept of being free and equal when it came to human beings, the nature of human beings – that of being egoistic and self-interested and the need for consent by participants in deciding how human beings should be regulated (state form) and how individuals should pursue their private affairs. Hobbes advocates a sovereign that is ultimately absolute but established by the authority conferred by the people (Macpherson, 1968) The sovereign's right of command and the subjects' duty of obedience is the result of consent.

John Locke (1632-1704) had different opinion on human beings' capacity to organise. He did not believe that organisation has necessarily to be under a sovereign state. Human beings can organise themselves and trust each other in such a way that the chaos Hobbes conceptualised can be avoided. He rejected the notion of a great leviathan that would control every social aspect, that would have an uncontested unity and establishing and enforcing laws according to the sovereign's will. According to Locke, the state/government should be for the defence of life, liberty, rights and property of its citizens (Dunn, 1969.) Inherent in this position are some key principles such as the right of individuals to have freedom, property and to participate in political affairs. These rights are God given and they need to be enshrined in the law. Government should thus be by consent and when it (government) does not live to the aspirations of the people it should be replaced. Locke believed in the separation of powers between the constitutional monarchy, which held executive powers while the law making powers remained in a parliamentary assembly. Locke was of the opinion that the creation of a political community or government was the task of all individuals if their future were to be secured. Thus, membership to this political community i.e. citizenship, was necessary, and it bestowed responsibilities and rights, duties and powers, constraints and liberties. Locke is regarded as a key contributor to the development of liberalism and prepared the way for the tradition of popular representative government.

Jeremy Bentham (1748-1832) and James Mill (1773-1836) are among the first advocates of liberal democracy (Held, 1989) and were influenced by the ideas of Hobbes and Locke. To them liberal democracy was associated with a political apparatus that would ensure accountability of the governors to the governed. Only through democratic government would there be satisfactory means for choosing, authorising and controlling political decisions commensurate with the interests of the mass of individuals. They believed that only through the secret ballot, competition between political leaders (representatives), elections, separation of powers and the liberty of the press, speech and public association could 'the interest of the community in general' be sustained (Bentham, 1960) In terms of accountability of those in public office, they believed that they should be under the control of the electorate who are by nature utility maximisers – (something that could lead to the abuse of office for personal gain). The way of achieving this was through elections which could reinstate or depose incumbents.

To these utilitarians, the free vote and the free market were necessary conditions for the development of human capacities. The political thinker who most involved himself with the development of human capacities was Mill's son, John Stuart Mill (1806-1873). He saw liberal democracy or representative government as a necessary condition for the attainment of this ideal. As Held notes, representative government was for him very important 'not just because it established boundaries for the pursuit of individual satisfaction, but because it was an important aspect of the free development of individuality. Participation in political life (voting, involvement in local administration and jury service) was vital for the creation of direct interest in government and consequently, a basis for an involved, informed and developing citizenry.' (Held,1989:17)

Mill Jr. considered representative government as an essential element in the preservation of liberty and reason. It is the most suitable mode of government for the enactment of laws consistent with the principle of liberty just as the free exchange of goods in the market place is the most appropriate way of maximising economic liberty and economic good. Initially, Mill was committed to *laissez-faire* economic policy but modified his views at a later stage. A system of representative democracy makes government accountable to the citizenry and creates wiser citizens capable of pursuing the public interest.

The works of Hobbes, Locke, Bentham and the two Mills greatly influenced the notion of the liberal democratic state in England and the United States. However, their views generated controversial debates. Different theories of the liberal democratic state have been propounded in both the US and the UK and the Western world in general. These include the variations conceived by different people as to what constitutes pluralism, and representation in general. This led to such theorists as Schumpeter, Lasswell, Truman and Dahl; and the 'liberal anarchist' views like those of Hayek and Nozick. The central tenets of the liberal democratic state are, nevertheless, different from the alternative – an alternative that proved impossible in the modern world – the 'direct' or 'participatory democracy' (REDET,1995).

(Schumpeter (1947), for example, does not believe that representative democracy is practicable – actually he sees it as being as illusory and unrealistic as was the participative democracy advocated by Rousseau. To him the idea of the convergence of the will of the people to form the common will is not realistic. This is more so when societies become complex, with differentiation and division of labour leading to each individual having a different set of preferences and ambitions. Furthermore, the tendency has been established which shows that the career politicians group themselves forming a triad of elites – political, economic and professional – in which the majority of the people are excluded. With such a situation, one cannot imagine of this "popular or general will." Schumpeter proposed that, given the impossibility of true representation and participation in modern, complex societies, democracy was only a means through which people conferred power to agents who would represent them without necessarily representing what the conferees want or are interested in. This democratic method is meant to 'produce government' through competitive struggle for the votes of the conferees. It is, therefore, important that there be competitive elections.

Representatives and representative government

In a representative government, problems can arise regarding the nature of the relationship between the representative and the electorate, own party and the government (local and central) during elections. There are a number of issues to be raised. For example, once elected, are representatives free to speak and act according to their own consciences, or do they act in such a way as to secure their re-election to office? Should they behave more like delegates or agents instead of true representatives, acting on instructions issued by their constituents? The relationship between the representative and the represented has to do with political factors and also depends on the situation on the ground. However, there have to be basic principles, regardless of whether they are upheld or not. This is why, with these questions being asked, Yves Meny notes that Western democracies have rejected the idea of a definite mandate binding on the representatives, but none has gone so far as to declare total autonomy for the representative (Meny, 1990).

In Britain, for example, this problem manifests itself in the relationship between the MP and the constituency party. First, theoretically it is generally accepted that an MP is indeed a representative who decides on issues according to his own judgment, who speaks and votes in parliament as he wishes. Secondly, an MP cannot be forced to resign. Thirdly, an MP is protected by the doctrine that it is a breach of parliamentary privilege for a group of constituents, or any other body, to seek to limit an MP's freedom of speech. He is only limited by his parliamentary party, and has to bear the consequences of any actions that offend this body.

If an MP wants to be re-elected he needs to appreciate the consequences of any actions that may offend his constituents, which is an essential basis of the democratic principle of representation. Additionally, the MP's local party organs and other key stakeholders like party officers, supporters and canvassers have power to influence the conduct of MP leading to MPs seeing themselves as receiving instructions from the constituency. However, this experience is not uncommon. The experience of Britain, for example, shows how the constituency associations (which play a key role in the nomination of party candidates for constituencies in the Conservative Party) and the Constituency Labour Party, supporters, canvassers and other influential actors have managed to dictate to their MP on what to support in parliament. As early as 1774, when Edmund Burke was faced with this problem he reacted by arguing that once an MP was elected he did not represent his constituency alone, but he represented the whole nation (Edmund Burke in a speech to the electors in Bristol, 3 November, 1774). The relationship between an MP and his/her constituency can be influenced by other factors as well, as Mushi, (in this volume) has indicated. He suggests that there are political structures, political culture and economic factors that impinge upon the efficacy of representation in any one political system. Under political structural factors, he mentions the party system, the political system – whether presidential or parliamentary (bi-cameral or uni-cameral), the electoral system and the distribution of power between the branches of government and in society as a whole. The political cultural factors would include the level of competence among the citizens, the MP's perception of his role and power, and the expectations of the constituents. The economic factors relate to the capability of the political system to respond to the demands of the population in terms of the resources needed.

The personality of an individual MP can be added as another factor. This is much so because different MPs choose the path they have taken for different reasons, either made public or kept secret. Although MPs are supposedly representatives of 'all' their constituents, there are factors that make them unrepresentative also. For example, one can only effectively address some of the issues and problems that come from the constituency, which means some problems from the constituents may not be addressed. This shows the divide between those who are 'all-rounders,' those who are specialists and those who are just happy being party loyalists, swinging to the tune of the party. But for most, it is the relations with their constituency, local party and local organisations that matter most and as such, tend to concentrate more on constituency problems. Against this background the following section of this paper shows Tanzania's experience as far as the election and performance of representatives are concerned.

The Tanzanian experience

Pre-independence Legislative Council
During the colonial and transition periods, the struggle against foreign rule conditioned the candidacy for membership of the Legislative Council. Supporters of the main nationalist party – the Tanganyika African National Union (TANU) – were readily accepted showing of interest in joining the Council rather than for their personal qualities. Only on one occasion was a member rejected by TANU and he made it to the Council by running as an independent candidate. During that particular period TANU focused two out of the several possible functions a political party should perform: (i) the structuring of the popular vote and (ii) the integration and mobilisation of the citizenry.

The 1965-1990 elections
On attainment of independence the organisational goal of the political parties changed. However, only one political party remained strong. The others, especially the African National Congress, were forced out

of politics by the various means that the government of the day deployed. The opposition parties were finally officially outlawed after a presidential commission's recommendations. The succession process became the main goal leading the development agenda as well as the consolidation of power. Given the promises made during the independence struggle, the first agenda came up almost immediately in the minds of politicians and the population was also expecting something in that direction. Power consolidation, on the other hand, was a natural outcome of a post-colonial state administration holding to the reigns of power lest the outside world as well as internal rivals see them as being inept. The way the representatives were picked changed with these developments. In order to make sure that party zealots were the only ones to go through once the other parties had been outlawed, TANU's National Executive Committee (NEC) retained the right to pick the two contestants for each constituency. In the earlier elections, this was done at the district level by the relevant party organs.

The role played by the district was to prepare the preferential list for the NEC to select without necessarily following the priority of the district. Party membership was therefore the key qualification in the 1965 elections, coupled with the condition of being 'system friendly'. Some argue that since the voters did not refuse to vote for the two candidates picked by the national-level party organs, they were in concurrence with the party (Okema, 1990.) But the question here is whether the voters were politically competent to challenge the party and the system – that of 'one-party democracy.'

The Arusha Declaration of 1967 set the ideological bearing for Tanzania. The Declaration was an attempt to redirect the development effort after the first years of independence proved ineffective on this particular front. The Declaration had a chapter on a Leadership Code targeting people in government and the parastatal sector, particularly after the nationalisation that followed the Declaration. All the *dos* and *don'ts* were listed in the code for those considered leaders in party terms. MPs were part of those covered by this code. The selection for the parliamentary seat contest by the party thus meant one was 'ideologically correct.' For the 1970 elections, therefore, prospecting candidates for parliamentary seats had to be committed to the policies of socialism and self-reliance.

In the 1975 elections the party went ahead and tightened its grip on who should go into parliament by first introducing an election manifesto and secondly, the introduction of regional seats. The latter were also used as a possible safety net for party supporters who could not make it to parliament through the constituency contests. According to Okema (1990:41), the former was, 'a manifestation of the growing control of the party for the candidates were now being instructed on what to tell the electorate'. Other qualifications carried over from the past elections remained in place.

The 1980 elections were similar to those of the 1975. The exception was that TANU and The Afro-Shiraz Party (ASP) had merged forming *Chama Cha Mapinduzi* (CCM) provided which had implications on how mainland and Isles representatives were picked. Also, the economic hardship that faced the electorate (due to factors not necessarily directly linked to parliament) led to high MPs turnover and the electorate linked their suffering to the weaknesses of the government and the parliament as part and parcel of it. In 1985 the regional seats were scrapped. Instead, women as a group became a pool for recruiting MPs. The other categories of MPs and the required qualifications remained.

The 1990 elections were held under the same system of one-party state although by now the demands for opening up the political space for other non-CCM actors were openly echoed. Political pluralism was expected after the 1986 economic liberalisation. The economic liberalisation came amid severe economic hardship, which led to disenchantment of most sections of the Tanzanian society. In fact, the economic crisis was one of the contributing factors to the demands for change in the management of the political and economic affairs in the country (Mukandala, 1997.) Despite these demands and the pressure from within and without the country, the elections were again held under the single party with all the characteristics of the earlier elections. In 1991, a commission was finally formed to gather opinions of Tanzanians as to whether Tanzania should adopt multiparty politics or not. The commission recommended that Tanzania should adopt a multiparty system despite the fact that about 80 per cent of those interviewed indicated that they would prefer the single party system. The recommendation was adopted and the general elections in 1995 saw the participation of 13 political parties.

Relationship between MPs and their parties

Political parties are powerful actors when the issue of representation comes up because, in practice, the theory of the representative's mandate is counter-balanced by the role played by the political parties. It is the political party in power that devises programmes and implements them (through governments), the representatives come in at the second stage – when these programmes are presented in parliament for approval. Another critical concern is that studies have shown that power keeps shifting from being popular to being concentrated in few hands. At another level is the concern that if power is not concentrated in a few, then there is the tendency to have it concentrated and shared between the various elites in society – political, military and economic. The relationship between MPs and their own political parties in Tanzania can be examined at two levels: the pre-1992 period and the post-1992 period. During the 1962 – 1992 period, MPs had to toe the party line at both constituency and national levels, especially if they wanted to maintain or increase their chances of being recommended for candidacy in the next elections, as well as keeping their seats in parliament. The process of recruiting candidates for the parliamentary seat contests was such that the local party organs were as influential as the national level organs, although the latter could veto decisions from the former. This was exemplified by the National Executive Committee picking candidates who did not top the preferential lists from the district party organs.

Those who did not toe the party line could easily lose their seats in parliament once they were suspended from the party, which meant there was no need to wait for another election for the rebel MPs to lose seats! Since there was no alternative way into parliament, many MPs were therefore submissive to party orders, policies and regulations. The case of 1968 when several MPs were dismissed from the party for questioning the party moves to relegate parliament to a second position after the party in policy making, among other things, is evidence to this relationship (Van Velzen and Sterkenbury, 1972). The MPs were defending the liberal democratic norm that parliament is the only state organ that can claim to be representative and, therefore, should be the supreme organ and not the party. As a result of being non-members, they also lost their parliamentary seats. MPs were, therefore, bound by the party line and were not expected to go against it.

The multiparty period requires that all members of parliament be members of a registered political party. This, by implication means that all members of parliament are indirectly coerced to be submissive to their relevant parties if at all they intend to remain MPs and they also want to keep alive their aspirations for re-election into parliament. The absence of a constitutional provision for independent candidates implies that there are possibilities that would-be rebel and outspoken MPs may have decided to 'shut their mouths' for the sake of keeping their jobs, as well as enhancing their chances of re-election.

When MPs were questioned about their relationship with their political parties in the survey carried out in the 1995-2000 multiparty parliament, many of them replied that they are responsible to the voters first before any other political actor. Table 7.1 shows the frequencies and percentages as to whom they think they are responsible to in the first place.

Table 7.1: Responses to the question – To whom should an MP be first accountable (the party, the voters or the government)?

First accountable to	Frequency	%
The party	16	16
The voters	53	53
Party and voters	18	18
Party and government	5	5
Don't know/other/NA	8	8
Total	100	100

While some 53 per cent believe that they should first be accountable to the voters, the second biggest percentage is that of a combination between voters and the party at 18 per cent. Only 16 per cent thought they should be first responsible to their party. On balance, one can understand why the majority thinks the voters are most crucial when it comes to the question of responsibility. First, there are many voters who are not members of any political party or who are not members of the same political party as the MP they voted for. Loyalty to the party, once one is elected, would mean alienating these supporters, who are needed in the subsequent elections. Further, as theory would have it, once elected an MP is the representative of all people i.e. voters in the constituency. Secondly, in multiparty political systems, political parties tend to be electoral machines during elections. Once the elections are over, the MP should be more engaged in mobilisation of the people and supervise implementation of policies rather than go on being involved in party politics at the constituency level. Thirdly, when it comes to the preferential votes in the selection of party candidates, the members of the relevant party – and who constitute the electoral forum – have a decisive vote on who goes through. Fourthly, it is possible that the party at constituency level is not so important, given the experience of the 1995 intra-party preferential elections. These were fraught with corruption. It was money rather policies, party preference or individual qualities that determined winners. One can afford to 'ignore' the local party organs in favour of the voters knowing that it is rare that the national organs overturn preferential vote results.

Furthermore, when it comes to accountability, the party has its clout also in determining the fate of its members, including MPs. This is why 18 per cent thought they should be accountable to both the voters and the party. Apparently, in practice one has to be accountable to both in one way or another and it is the issue at stake that determines which point should be the first as far as accountability is concerned. Since the party is supporting the MP in his activities, it cannot be ignored. Table 7.2 below shows that political parties do support and help their MPs as they go about doing their representation job.

Table 7.2: Responses to the question – Does your party support you at the constituency level?

Response	Frequency	Percentage
It helps	72	72
It somehow helps	18	18
It does not help/blocks	5	5
Others/NA	5	5
Total	100	100

The data shows that 90 per cent of the MPs in the sample believe that their parties do help them in their constituencies. Research has indicated that political parties support their MPs by, among other things, setting policies, offering to cooperate with MPs in their daily business, mobilising people in constituencies when it comes to development activities and providing information. The same applies to parties at national level where 91 per cent of the sampled MPs indicated that they received cooperation and help from their national party offices (see Table 7.3 below). A small percentage of MPs (five per cent) did indicate that they do not receive any help from their national party offices. The same applies to constituency-level party organs where three per cent said they did not receive any help. All happen to be MPs on the ruling party ticket. Nobody from the opposition parties failed to receive constituency-level support from their parties.

Table 7.3: Responses to the question – Does your party at national level support you?

Responses	Frequency	%
It helps	91	91
It does not help at all	5	5
It blocks	2	2
NA/other	2	2
Total	100	100

There are cases also of political parties blocking efforts of the MP in his/her constituency. This has affected two per cent of the sampled MPs. This is mainly due to lack of cooperation, lack of consultation and sometimes parties encouraging the people not to cooperate with the MP. Given the crises that faced some of the opposition parties like the one in NCCR, it would not be strange to find that party organs campaign for non-cooperation with MPs who have gone against national party leaders or other party structures.

The high percentages of parties supporting their MPs is demonstrated by who gets the praise when constituency matters are well attended. When there are good services, it is the MP's political party that gets the credit. Although some MPs bring change through individual effort and enterprise, only four per cent of the sampled MPs felt that when there is praise and appreciation it is theirs. This is compared to 73 per cent who said that it is their party that carries the credit for jobs well done in their constituencies (see Table 7.4 below). 7 per cent thought that it is the government in general which should gets the credit.

Table 7.4: Responses to the question – Who is praised when constituency matters are well attended to?

Responses	Frequency	%
The MP	4	4
The MP's party	73	73
The government	7	7
The constituency voters	5	5
Tanzania	3	3
Other responses	6	6
Don't know/NA	2	2

The relationship between MPs and the government

The government is empowered to collect taxes and other resources which are again redistributed to different competing demands in ministries, regions, and districts/constituencies. The MP participates in presenting the needs of his constituency to the central government for allocation of resources to solve the problems. For example, at regional level, MPs are members of the Regional Consultative Committee whose functions include the provision of 'advice to local government authorities regarding their development plans,' and 'monitoring and ensuring the coordination of the overall economic development in the region' (See United Republic of Tanzania, *The Regional Administration Act, 1997, item 11 (a) and (e))*. MPs also sit in the district councils whose functions include the maintenance and facilitation of law and order and the promotion of social welfare and economic well-being of all persons in the council area. The MP is, therefore, an actor in both central and local government.

One of the questions that the sampled MPs were asked was whether the local authorities covering their constituencies were helpful to them or not. The answers to the question are summarised in Table 7.5.

Table 7.5: Responses to the question – Is your local authority in your constituency supportive?

Responses	Frequency	%
It helps	39	39
It somehow helps	23	23
It doesn't help/It blocks	15	15
Other responses	22	22
NA/missing	1	1
Total	100	100

If we combine the 'it helps' and 'it somehow helps' the percentage comes to 62, which is significant. It seems local authorities do help many MPs in their duties as representatives of the people. However, 15 per cent of the respondents indicated that the local authorities in their areas were not helpful, and in some cases they blocked their efforts. Out of these 15 MPs 8 (8 per cent of the total sample and all from the opposition) indicated that their efforts were actually blocked by the local authorities. Three out of the five who said the authorities were not helpful are from the opposition parties. Therefore, out of the 15 per cent that had difficulties with the authorities, 13 per cent is the share of the opposition parties. This can be explained by the fact that in many district, municipal and city councils, the ruling party (CCM) has the majority of the councilors. Opposition MPs find it very difficult to have their proposals passed by these councillors. A good example is Mbeya Municipal Council where there was an opposition MP and a council of 36 elected councillors, only three of whom were from the opposition.

The statistical distribution of the 15 per cent between the mainland and Zanzibar can be seen in Table 7.6.

Table 7.6: The distribution of the per cent of 'don't help' and 'blocks' between Mainland and Zanzibar

	Zanzibar	Mainland
It does not help	3	2
It blocks	6	4
Total	9	6

In terms of geographical distribution, nine out of 22 MPs from Zanzibar have problems with the local authorities, which accounts for about 41 per cent. On the other hand, out of 77 Mainland MPs only six or around eight per cent had problems with their local authorities.

Table 7.7: Responses to the question – Does the central government help/support you in the constituency?

Responses	Frequency	%
It helps	33	33
It somehow helps	28	28
It doesn't help/blocks	10	10
Other responses	27	27
NA/missing	1	1
Total	100	100

The pattern of the relationship between MPs and the central government is similar to that of the local authorities in that 61 per cent find the government helpful (compared to 62 per cent for local authorities). Table 7.7 shows, however, that the level of being unhelpful is lower when it comes to the central government which is at 10 per cent compared to 15 per cent of the local authorities.

Relationship between MPs and voters

The cooperation an MP is likely to get from the voters can be alluded to the MP's personal appeal and efforts in solving the constituency's problems, with some influence from the party he represents. There is thus the influence of party image as well as the image of the MP himself/herself. Party image stands for the general impression of a voter on a political party based on the party policies, successes and/or failures, general conduct of members and leaders, and party potential. The results of the survey show an overwhelmingly positive picture when it comes to voters support to their MPs as Table 7.8 shows.

Table 7.8: Responses to the question – Are your voters helpful?

Responses	Frequency	%
They help	86	86
They are somehow helpful	9	9
They block	1	1
Other responses	3	3
NA/missing	1	1
Total	100	100

If we combine 'they help' and 'somehow helpful' we get a high percentage of 95 signifying that once the people elect their MP they tend to cooperate with him/her in order to bring about development in their constituency.

The same picture emerges when one considers organised interests in the constituency. The MPs were for example asked whether NGOs and other organisations were agents of change and whether they (MPs) had good co-operation. The majority of MPs (80 per cent) categorically indicated they received some kind of help (support, facilities, lobbying, etc.) from the local NGOs and other associations as indicated in Table 7.9.

Where NGOs exist, they have helped in various development activities in the constituencies they are located. These range from loans to women and youth, water and road improvement projects, school buildings, caring for orphans, to recreational activities. The pattern between the ruling and the opposition parties as far as this variable is concerned is the same, except that the opposition parties did not indicate that there were associations or NGOs that lobbied for them.

Table 7.9: Local associations and NGOs support to the MP

Type of support	Frequency	%
Facilities	13	13
Lobbying	3	3
Facilities/lobbying/support	53	53
Political support	11	11
Depends on association/NGO	1	1
Depends: permission, attitude, experience, etc.	4	4
Other answers	15	15

The pattern between Zanzibar and the mainland is also similar i.e. the associations and NGOs have been supportive and very helpful to the respondents. However, we need to point out here that in some areas, NGOs, especially those which are activist by nature, have come into conflict with politicians including MPs. Those NGOs which are educative and mainly sensitisation-oriented have been seen as a threat to politicians in that they make the citizen more 'demanding' to the local politicians. But when it comes to those which can mobilise own resources and use these resources in the constituencies for development projects, then these are welcome and praised by local politicians. We believe the second category of NGOs are the ones which the sampled MPs were particularly referring to.

Since these NGOs contribute to the social, economic or political development in the constituency, the MPs have been obliged to acknowledge their (NGOs) efforts by using different gestures, probably to keep the relation alive for future cooperation. These gestures are indicated in Table 7.10. Thanking the associations verbally and in writing has been picked as the most common gesture. However, 13 respondents never received assistance for their constituencies from associations or NGOs and these were probably part of the 43 respondents (43 per cent) who indicated that there are either no such associations in their constituencies or if they are there they never offered any help.

Table 7.10: Gestures of appreciation to NGOs and associations

Type of gesture	Rank & frequencies		
	1st	2nd	3rd
Appreciate in writing or verbally	45	17	5
Invitations	3	5	2
Project inspection	7	9	6
Visiting them	3	6	5
Educate voters on the associations	2	2	1
Utilize assistance efficiently	1	6	2
Morally supporting them	2	-	-
Ensure sustainability of projects	3	3	4
Award prizes	-	1	3
Involve them in activities	-	2	-
Give feedback	-	-	4
No response/DK/none	17	44	65
No aid offered	13	-	-

Conclusion

Many Tanzanian representatives, like many others elsewhere in the world, respond to a political culture and the prevailing rules of the political game. The Tanzanian MP relates to the electorate, his/her party and the current government because these are important actors in his/her career. The electorate votes MPs into parliament, parties choose the parliamentary candidates, and the government (central and local) is the vehicle through which MPs can hope to deliver political goods. The majority of MPs believe, however, that they are first and foremost accountable to the electorate any other actor. Ideally, before this is the correct stand because MPs represent and should be answerable, to the people. But, in practice, it seems all the three actors play key roles in the choosing and functioning of MPs.

The party – especially the party central office – can overturn decisions made by the constituency party in the initial short-listing of candidates. Thus, in the case of Tanzania where independent candidates are not allowed to stand, it is necessary for politicians to maintain good relations with their own parties. The voters choose who finally goes to parliament and therefore, MPs must maintain good relations especially if they intend to run for the office again. Lastly, the government is instrumental because it controls the resources. During the implementation of programmes, the government and MPs need to cooperate closely for both partners to improve their future re-election prospects.

Parliaments have three functions: representation, legislation and the control of the executive. This chapter looked at the representative function and the relationships between the representatives, the represented, the parties that nominated them and the government of the day. The representative function has undergone transformation over the centuries and actual representation has not always matched the ideal. For this reason some people have tended to see defects in the nature of the representation in the modern world.

The nature of representation in Tanzania may be even more defective than that in Western democracies due to the weaknesses of its supporting infrastructure. Factors such as illiteracy, uncontrollable corruption, misuse of power and public property by incumbents, and lack of transparency can make a representative system a farce. However, with time given the role played by the private mass media and other developments, the representation system will gradually become more responsive to the needs and aspirations of the electorate.

References

Bentham, J. (1960). *Fragment Government*, Oxford: Blackwell.
Dunn, J.(1969). *The Political Thought of John Locke*, Cambridge: CUP.
Held, D. (1989). 'Introduction' in Held, *et al* (eds). *States and Societies*, Oxford: Basil Blackwell.
Macpherson, C.P (ed.), (1968). *Leviathan*. Harmondsworth: Penguin.
Meny, Y. (1990). *Comparative Government in Western Europe: Britain, France, Italy, and Western Germany*, Oxford: OUP.
Mukandala, R.(1997). "Background to the 1995 General Election: Constitutional Changes and Political Liberalization", in *TEMCO The 1995 General Elections in Tanzania*, Dar es Salaam: Dar es Salaam Election Monitoring Committee
Mushi, S.(1999). "The Role of the Members of Parliament as Representatives of the People" A paper submitted to REDET, University of Dar es Salaam.
Okema, M.(1990). "Some Salient Changes in the Tanzanian Parliamentary System", in H. Othman, I. Buva and M. Okema (eds) *Tanzania: Democracy in Transition*, Dar es Salaam: DUP
Pateman, C. (1970). *Participation and Democratic Theory*, Cambridge: CUP.
Plamenatz, J. (1963). *Man and Society*, Vol. 1, London: Longman.
REDET (1995). *The Foundation of Democracy*, Dar es Salaam: DUP
Schumpter, (1947). *Capitalism, Socialism, and Democracy*, London: Allen and Urwin.
Van Velzen, H.U.T., and Sterkenburg, J.J. (1972), "Strings in the Tanzanian National Assembly", I.L Cliffe and J.S. Saul, (eds), *Socialism in Tanzania*, in Nairobi: EAPH.

8

Lobbying the Parliament in Tanzania: Structures and Processes

Amon E. Chaligha

Introduction

Lobbying parliament is an essential ingredient of parliamentary multiparty democracy. In many countries there is a tendency for citizens and/or citizen organisations to lobby only the executive branch of government, namely the president and his cabinet. The result is that parliament is undermined. Laws may be proposed by the government and passed without much input from concerned citizens, experts and organised groups.

Lobbying parliament is an attempt made by individuals and organised groups to influence parliamentary deliberations and decisions. Ford (1996:14) defines lobbying as the process of achieving public policy goals, most often of private interest, through the selected application of political pressure In this instance, lobbyists play a constructive role in policy presentation and participation, alerting elected representatives to particular issues and providing detailed technical and legislative advice. In this paper, lobbying is used in a wider sense to describe any formal and informal approaches made to members of parliament by any individual or organised group, for the express purpose of influencing decisions made by parliament in the course of fulfilling its legislative responsibility.

Lobbying is and remains an important instrument of representative democracy. Why so? Simply because, as Stewart (1958:210) argues, without lobbying.activities many people would probably not know of the threats posed by a certain bill on their rights/interests, and hence take no action is taken to safeguard those rights/interests. Lobbyists therefore raise the consciousness of both the representatives and electorate. Members of parliament are frequently reminded of their obligations by lobbyists, while the non-attentive public is woken up and is sensitised about what actions need to be taken to keep constant contact with their representatives.

Lord Thompson (1996:13), a renowned British member of parliament, has also argued that 'lobbying, done properly, is a perfectly honorable democratic activity [which can help members of parliament] better judge where the public interest finally lies if the rival lobbyists have presented their case with professional skill.' This means that parliament has to design mechanisms for involving various elements of society in order to realise its potential. However, lobbying does not preclude the fact that members of parliament are 'influenced by general arguments from their constituencies and from the country as a whole' (Budgen, 1996:12). Essentially, parliament has to involve both constituents as well as professionals to enrich its deliberations.

It has also to be pointed out that since 'lobbying is about influence not power (lobbying) must be seen as open, honest and democratic' (Mendelssohn, 1996:11). Lobbying should therefore take place in a more formalised manner to ensure openness and accountability in public policy formulation by parliament. Information presented by lobbyists must generally be perceived to be accurate and well researched. 'Officials emphasize that information must be reliable not only because they need it for their own decisions, but also because they use this information in communications with other officials and with the public.' (Milbrath, 1970:376) Inaccurate information may mislead a member of parliament. Decisions made using such information may prove to be embarrassing to the individual member of parliament as well as to the whole parliament. The integrity of the lobbyist as well as that of the legislature may suffer.

It can also be argued that lobbying 'creates a system of functional representation, which operates alongside electoral representation and as such, lobbyists greatly increase the amount of and quality of information available to governments ... thus, partly redress one of the defects of democracy, because they reflect the quality or intensity of concern.' (Hague, et.al. 1992:222) The defect in point emanates from the fact that citizens are almost certainly consulted only during elections when they are asked to pick their representatives. However, after elections, their representatives in parliament rarely consult them. Nevertheless, because of their expertise and dedication in a cause they stand for, lobbyists are in essence able to take up the cause of various members of society not directly represented in parliament.

Burrell (1996:10) argues further that 'lobbying is an integral element of any truly democratic society; the existence of strong collective organisations bridging the gap between the individual and the authorities is a key feature which distinguishes a free society from a totalitarian one.' Under such conditions Tanzania cannot afford to ignore the importance of the lobbying in mechanism in widening the scope of parliamentary democracy. We are aware that to-date people lobby individual parliamentarians but do not lobby parliament. Lobbying is precariously done under stealthy conditions. There is need to formalise lobbying of the parliament and make it one of the pillars of democracy in Tanzania.

Indeed, the government as a whole hopes that 'in exchange for a say in policy-making, pressure groups will support measures passed; cooperate in their implementation; accept the authority of government; respect the confidentiality of discussions and behave in a responsible fashion.' (Burrell 1996:189) Parliamentary decisions gain credence when they are seen to have included inputs from all sectors of society. Parliament cannot claim to have the monopoly of knowledge. Frequent consultations with those who are affected by parliamentary decisions are therefore of paramount importance.

Consultation with organised groups is of paramount importance to backbench Members of parliament mostly because they lack specialised information on most policy issues presented by the government. Msekwa (1995:87) has pointed out that:

> 'Whereas Ministers are supported by the whole administrative machine and are briefed by professional civil servants for every prepared speech and every prepared answer to a parliamentary question, the backbencher is mostly on his/her own, lacking facilities for research and having no access to government files. He/she is therefore unlikely to be an expert on any subject unless he/she happens to have personal experience of it, either through his/her

own professional training or through relevant past work experience.'
(Msekwa 1995:87)

In order for the backbencher to counter government arguments and make it more accountable for its actions, there is need for parliament to seek specialised information from the professionals, organised groups and all those who will be affected by parliamentary decisions.

Ideally, the relationship between citizens, professionals and other organised groups and parliament should be that of mutual cooperation and consultation. This point is underscored by Ball (1971:110) when he stresses that 'governments want advice, technical information and most of all cooperation from strong interest groups.' This cooperation between parliament and 'organised groups' has to be institutionalised first to give these groups the recognised right to be consulted and second, ensure that these consultations do not give them undue influence over parliamentary policy formulating process. The question then is how can this cooperation be institutionalised?

In a parliamentary form of government, organised groups have more difficulty in influencing the legislature than in a presidential system. According to Raj (1990:187), the main reason for these difficulties is the fact that parliamentary forms of government tend to be run on the basis of party strength in parliament. Their difficulties increase when party discipline is strict.

In party dominated political systems, the chief executive also often doubles as the party boss, who normally presides over party caucuses that pick parliamentary candidates. A member of parliament may therefore not find it expedient to oppose bills favoured by the executive. Furthermore, the chief executive presides over the disbursement of financial resources, some of which may be useful during elections. The executive also determines government business in parliament. All signals indicate that in party dominated government systems, the centre of action resides with the executive rather than the legislature.

Organised groups are aware of the futile effort to concentrate on lobbying parliament under such circumstances. They therefore tend to direct their efforts to the president/prime Minister and the various government ministers and other senior civil servants of the executive branch of government. This observation is not in any way meant to assume that organised groups will ignore parliament completely. They can only do so at their own peril. Parliament is far too important an institution to ignore. However, in party dominated systems and other similar political systems where strict party discipline is the norm, organised groups continue to lobby parliament in order to sustain gains made with the executive or mitigate their differences.

Organised groups in party dominated political systems have 'the greatest chance of influencing legislation in Parliament when the normal party alignment is broken. If there is dissention among Government backbenchers with regard to a particular aspect of Government policy, this can be exploited by the opponents of the policy' (Punnet, 1994:154). Moreover, most organised groups know that if they are persistent on their pursuits regarding government legislation the government is likely to relent. All they have to do is to use effective lobbying tactics to convince the government that their case is a valid one. As Punnet (1994:155) has further observed:

> 'In the passage of legislation through Parliament the Government may make concessions to the views of interested parties in order to placate the interest groups, or through fear of losing electoral or financial support. On the other hand, it may be that during the passage of a Bill the Government may become convinced that the pressure group's case is a valid one.' (Punnet, 1994:155)

It is imperative, however, for organised groups to avoid lobbying tactics that may give the impression of undue influence to members of parliament. Tactics that threaten to withdraw electoral support or threaten the life of a member of parliament because of his position on a certain bill constitute a breach of parliamentary privilege. Such methods are also undesirable because they tend to undermine the basic human and constitutional rights of an MP to be entitled to his own opinion. Nor is it politically desirable for organised groups to buy the support of Members of Parliament.

Lobbying processes

It is generally understood that organised groups use both direct and indirect methods to communicate with the legislature. 'Some direct methods are personal presentations of viewpoints and research findings, and testimony at hearings. Some indirect methods are approaches through constituents and friends, letter and telegram campaigns, public relations campaigns and the publicising of voting records,' of individual members in the legislature. These methods will be discussed in more detail below.

Committee hearings

Committee hearings create a golden opportunity for establishing formal communication procedures by the legislature. Thus, the legislature can establish various standing committees the number of which may be determined by the number of government ministries. The importance of legislative committees has been well articulated by Raj (1990:191) when he asserts that:

> 'Since legislatures are over worked and have no technical expertise to legislate on the subjects which are introduced in every session of Parliament, much of the work, both in parliamentary and Presidential democracies, is dealt with at the committee stage. Usually the House accepts committee recommendations'.

Organised groups are aware of these advantages and find it expedient to make direct presentations of their viewpoints to the legislature in the manner of committee hearings. Furthermore, these groups realise that 'it is far easy to convince few members in the committee than the House as a whole.' Given that before the full legislature discusses any government proposal for legislation the relevant parliamentary committee discusses it in the first reading, it is imperative for organised groups to target parliamentary committee members. Hence, their efforts to attend committee hearings is a deliberate effort to influence public policy formulation.

Parliamentary committees usually invite members of the public to appear before a standing committee and give expert testimony on government bills or policy proposals. Specific invitations are normally sent to those organised groups that will be affected by the bill under discussion. Various subject matter experts and practitioners can also be invited to give expert advice on the efficacy of the bill. The intensity of committee hearings and the degree of consultation with organised groups vary from country to country. There is a tendency for more committee consultations where the committees themselves are powerful enough to amend or reject any bill under discussion.

According to Milbrath (1970:388):

> 'Committee hearings are a formal communication procedure provided by congressional committees and some independent regulatory missions. They are available to nearly anyone wanting to present his point of view. Not only do congressional committees feel compelled to hold hearings on every major bill, but also all lobby groups concerned feel compelled to testify. Committees fear criticism from groups and individuals, hence all invites are usually heard at open hearings'.

Committees can also call expert testimony from any individual specialised in the subject under its scrutiny. The function of the committee hearing is to help the legislators to appreciate and crystallise the full implications of the bill set before them. Moreover, during the committee hearings, 'legislators and lobbyists have the opportunity to arrive at a rough estimate of the intensity of support or opposition and to locate the various coalitions which have invariably been formed (Zeigler and Peak, 1972:140)'.

Presentation of research results

Research results are considered an important lobbying tactic in the United States, where 'lobbyists in most roles rank research second or third among the 14 tactics. Legislative staff persons are notable exceptions, however; they rate research high but rate other tactics such as collaboration, constituent contact, hearings and letters, higher' (Milbrath, 1970:386).

Research, if conducted properly, can provide information to assist legislators to make informed decisions. Organised groups often make research reports an integral part of their presentation in committee hearings. Thus, when Congress invites comments and advice from the public on a bill before a congressional committee, lobbyists often make available their research findings to the committee. Lobbyists also defend interests of their clients before congressional committees with data from their various researches. However, some organised groups make it their habit to present any research findings to individual legislators, especially those in whose constituencies the group conducts the research. Specialised organisations prefer to make their impact on the legislators by presentation of their research findings.

Another effective way to present research findings is through seminars and lunch or dinner talks. Organised groups can arrange seminars for members of parliament where research findings can be disseminated to them. However, some organised groups like to influence the legislators by presenting them with research findings during working lunch or dinner talks attended by targeted legislators. Lunch or dinner talks are preferred because most legislators have busy schedules. These talks are often informal, which makes the legislators relaxed but attentive.

It is also important to point out that legislators are influenced by quality research findings. This is because keen legislators prefer to work with ideas and information that is backed by facts and figures from research. However, research results have to be carefully judged in terms of proven methodology used and in terms of the reputation and competence of the researcher.

Action committees
Concerned citizens may establish action committees. Citizens may, through these action committees, calls the attention of the mass media to discuss pertinent issues in their constituency. Later, the action committee may transform into a political lobby and strive to influence legislation. Action committees are often single-issue lobbies.

A typical action committee comes into being when some concerned citizens decide to organise against government decisions considered to be contrary to their convictions and interests. For example, if the government decides to introduce legislation that will legalise abortion, a group of concerned moralists may make petitions and rallies against such decisions by forming an anti-abortion lobby. This lobby can then target some members of parliament in order to exert pressure to their colleagues in an effort to defeat the government bill.

Action committees are also referred to as 'citizens' committees'. These are used to put pressure on legislators to support certain bills. Interested officials who have a stake in the policy or bill under consideration in the legislature initiate some citizen committees. Citizen committees are used to stimulate and organise the support of lobby groups.

Mass lobbying

The main objective of this method is to convince the member of parliament of 'the degree of feeling in his constituency on an issue and incidentally to put some argument to him' (Stewart, 1958:207). In a mass lobby, organised groups marshal the support of several hundreds of people and ask them to march and flood the corridors of parliament and demand to see their members of parliament. Organised groups may, therefore, 'organise a mass lobbying of an MP by his constituents, or a mass demonstration at Westminster' This kind of lobbying structure is not very useful, as the crowds may sometimes become unruly and uncontrollable.

Personal lobbying

Personal lobbying is another effective means of persuading a member of parliament. According to Milbrath (1970:377), personal lobbying means 'lobbyists normally present their views personally by paying visits to governmental decision-makers and delivering their messages in face-to-face conversations. They sometimes deliver messages over the phone or via a written letter or memo.' Most lobbyists believe that a 'direct personal visit by an envoy is more effective than written communication in gaining access. Message delivered in person can be more fully elaborated, and is more likely to reach a decision-maker when he is in a receptive frame of mind.' (Milbrath, 1970:378)

These advantages make this lobbying process the preference of organised groups that send their representatives to meet a targeted member of parliament. Such officials approach members of parliament for pre-arranged meetings. Both sides prepare for the meeting, thereby ensuring success. It is in this spirit that some organised groups have full time parliamentary agents or parliamentary correspondents to maintain contact with their local MPs. However, too many personal envoys from organised groups may create unintended inconveniences to targeted MPs. Furthermore, competition for attention from these personal envoys means less guarantee for winning the support of the MPs.

Lobbying parliament in Tanzania

In Tanzania organised groups lobby individual members of parliament. However, lobbying is not formally institutionalised in Tanzania. Rather lobbying is haphazardly done. Whereas the various organised groups can formally lobby the executive branch of government, they have no mechanism to formally lobby parliament. The result is such that parliament can pass laws which affect these organisations without consulting them, hence creating animosity between them and the parliament. Parliament is also denied the advantage of gaining access to expert information and advice, so important in aiding quality debates in parliament, a crucial factor in passing workable and acceptable legislation.

Lobbying parliament assumes that parliament is supreme and therefore, it is able to make policy decisions that affect society. In the first few years of independence parliament was supreme in Tanganyika. President Nyerere recognised this fact, in his address to parliament on 25 April, 1964, when he requested it to ratify the Articles of Union between Zanzibar and Tanganyika. In recognition of the supremacy of parliament, President Nyerere is quoted by Msekwa (1995:17) as having stated that:

> 'This Parliament is the supreme organ of the people of Tanganyika. Any one or any group of persons other than this Assembly can, finally decide no important constitutional issues, or important matter concerning state agreements. All such matters must be brought before this house and it is entirely in your discretion, Hon. Members, to approve them or reject them'.

It can, however, be pointed out that this parliamentary supremacy did not last long. The 1965 Constitutional Amendments that ushered in the era of a one party state in Tanzania eroded this supremacy in favour of party supremacy. Several MPs opposed these constitutional changes and paid dearly. According to Pius Msekwa (1995:20), 'at its meeting held in Tanga in the middle of October, 1968, the NEC expelled seven MPs from the Party for having grossly violated the Party creed both in their attitudes and in their actions and for showing very clear opposition to the party and its policies. The expulsion from the Party carried with it automatic loss of their parliamentary seats. The ruling Party's NEC also resolved in this meeting that all policy decisions would in future be submitted first to NEC for consideration and approval, before being submitted to parliament for legislative enactment. President Nyerere himself later confirmed the supremacy of the ruling party over the parliament, in February 1974, when he stated clearly that:

> 'Under our One Party Constitution, TANU is supreme. It is able to give directions to the Government about the general policy that must be adopted for national development and it has power to give specific instructions about priorities of action in any aspect of our national life. (Msekwa, 1995:22)'

Under such political conditions it is no wonder that organised groups have been used to lobby the party and the government rather than the parliament. However, with the introduction of multiparty politics in 1992 and further constitutional changes in 1993, the supremacy of parliament has been somewhat restored, at least on paper. Section 63, (2), of the Constitution of the United Republic of Tanzania reiterates this supremacy by stating that:

> 'The National Assembly shall be the principal organ of the United Republic which shall, on behalf of the people, supervise and advise the Government of the United Republic and all its agencies in the exercise of their functions in accordance with this Constitution.'
> (*Jamuhuri ya Muungano wa Tanzania,* 1995 a: 61)

The 1993 Constitutional Amendments removed all sections giving the ruling party supremacy over the parliament. Parliament is now in a better position to fulfill its constitutional obligation to supervise and advise the government and its agencies. This can be fulfilled if parliament can draw inputs from organised groups and specialized individuals within the country. In this context one would expect increased efforts to lobby parliament.

Standing orders and rules of procedure

Parliamentary standing orders and rules of procedure give parliamentary standing committees powers to invite any person to give expert testimony on any issue. Thus, section 88, (6), of these standing orders (unofficial translation) states in part that each standing committee of parliament 'can allow people who are not members of parliament to attend and participate in committee business, but they will not be allowed to vote.' (*Jamuhuri ya Muungano wa Tanzania*, 1995b: 40) Indeed, this standing order can be the basis for lobbying parliament in Tanzania.

Furthermore, any parliamentary standing committee that is investigating the conduct of government business has legal authority to call any witnesses before it. According to Msekwa, (1995) the Parliamentary Immunities, Powers and Privileges Act, 1988 (No. 3 of 1988) empowers any standing committee of Parliament to 'order any person to attend before it and to give evidence – or to produce any document in the possession of, or under the control of such person.' Armed with such legal backing there is no reason why the Tanzanian parliament should not be able to formalise lobbying in Tanzania.

It may nevertheless be pointed out that, some organised groups have made some efforts to lobby parliament. Such efforts have been limited to few public corporations that have lobbied individual members of parliament to assist them in fighting off government measures against their privileges. Thus, in 1995 the National Insurance Corporation (NIC) successfully lobbied parliament to reject a government proposal to privatise the insurance business in Tanzania. Because of vocal opposition from members of parliament the government was forced to withdraw the bill which aimed at ending NIC's monopoly of insurance business. If formal lobbying had been allowed at the committee stage, government embarrassment could have been avoided.

Position of organised groups on lobbying parliament

Interviews with various people representing organised groups reveals that lobbying is gaining ground in Tanzania. About 30 organisations were consulted. The respondents were asked: 'If you have a problem that requires government action whom do you normally see for a solution: the president, the minister, the principal secretary, or your member of parliament?' It is interesting to observe that about 11 per cent of the respondents said they saw the president, while about 25.9 per cent saw the minister responsible for the sector, 55.5 per cent saw the principal secretary and only 7.4 per cent saw their member of parliament. Given that the president, the principal secretary and the sectoral minister belong to the executive branch of government, it means that 92.6 per cent of the respondents preferred to lobby the executive branch of government while only 7.4 per cent lobbied parliament. When they were asked why they preferred to lobby the executive branch of government, most respondents said they did so because it is the branch of government that has money. The executive is therefore accorded a higher status than parliament.

Senior government officials patronise some organised groups. Tanzania Legion, for example, said, 'the President of Tanzania is our Patron; if we have a problem we inform our patron who can show us where to go.' On the other hand, Dar es Salaam Chamber of Commerce said that depending on the magnitude and nature of the problem 'we can go to the principal secretary of the ministry from which the problem originates and to the principal secretary of any ministry which we think can help us.' Other organised groups would only go to the minister or even the president, after the principal secretary responsible for the ministry has 'failed to leave up to our expectations.' Most considered parliament as unable to help them. Occasionally, organised groups go to any member of parliament, who appears sympathetic to their cause (The Confederation of Tanzanian Industries (CTI), The Tanzanian Chamber of Commerce, Industry and Agriculture (TCCIA), Washirika, etc.,).

Public organised groups would only go to parliament after first consulting their respective boards and their parent ministries. However, if they consider the parent ministry antagonistic to the welfare of the corporation, they lobby individual members of parliament who appear vocal and sympathetic.

Respondents were also asked: 'If the government makes proposals for changing laws, or budget proposals, tax changes that may affect your members, are you consulted?' Seven respondents (25.9 per cent) said they are consulted, while 20 respondents (74.1 per cent) said they are not consulted. Most of those who said they are consulted are the chambers of commerce, such as Dar es Salaam Chamber of Commerce, CTI and TCCIA who said they were consulted in the 1996/97 Budget proposal. One senior official of The Dar es Salaam Chamber of Commerce acknowledges that:

'For the first time, we have been consulted. Our chairman participated in the committee that presented and discussed many things that were announced by the Minister of Finance in his 1996/97 Budget proposal'.

The Tanzania Chamber of Commerce, Industry and Agriculture and the Confederation of Tanzania Industries prepared position papers, which were presented to the government as inputs to the 1996/97 budget proposals. Prof. Samuel Wangwe, the Executive Director of the Economic and Social Research Foundation (ESRF), submitted the private sector's first draft taxation proposals to the Ministry of Finance and the Planning Commission in his capacity as chairman of the drafting committee. The report contained proposals on how to improve tax collection and on how to reduce tax rates and the multiplicity of taxes (*Daily News*, 6 May 1996.)

The Tanzania Employers Association (ATE) and the Tanzania Federation of Free Trade Unions (TFTU) have frequent consultation with the government. Both argue that they are frequently consulted because Tanzania has ratified Article 144 of the International Labour Organisation (ILO) convention which requires that labour industrial relations have to be based on 'tripartite' consultations between the government, employers associations and labour unions. Over and above these regular consultations, TFTU also lobbies members of parliament who used to be trade union leaders in the past.

Respondents were also asked whether they maintain any contact with parliament and if so, what type of contact? All respondents said they do not maintain any direct (formal) contact with parliament on a regular basis. However, most said they do get in touch with individual members of parliament whenever they have an issue that the government appears adamant to pursue contrary to the interests of their members.

When asked if there is any member of parliament who is sympathetic to 'your institution' and what makes them believe that this member of parliament can help them in parliament, only five out of 27 (18.5 per cent) organised groups consulted in this study answered in the affirmative. The Chambers of Commerce have several members of parliament still holding positions in the chamber by virtue of being prominent owners of several businesses and industries. The trade unions also believe that former trade unionists in parliament are sympathetic to their cause and can consult them when the need arises. It is apparent that for those organised groups that believe they have somebody to fall back to in parliament it is because of class interests. Either these MPs have businesses of their own, or they come from the rank and file of union leadership.

Organised groups were also asked whether they would like to maintain dialogue with parliament and how they would like this dialogue to take place. All the 27 (100 per cent) organisations that cooperated with the researcher said they would like to maintain continuous dialogue with parliament. They think that if parliament wants to be successful in its deliberations, then it has to consult with all the relevant organised groups.

The form of contact preferred is direct consultation whenever the government presents to parliament any legislation or policy proposal or international agreement for ratification with ramifications to the members of the organised groups. These consultations have to be formal and institutionalised by being recognised by protocol that makes it mandatory for parliament to consult any organised group that will be affected by its decision. For these consultations to be meaningful, they have to make a difference not only in the parliamentary debates, but also in substantial changes to the original government proposal.

Organised groups would like to have easy access to the member of parliament in their constituency. They would like the local member of parliament to develop a habit of consulting them, by phone or letters asking them about problems that undermine the welfare of their members. However, a few major organised groups, especially the chambers of commerce, said they can influence members of parliament by organising seminars and inviting them to take part. The Confederation of Tanzania Industries organised one such seminar for the parliamentary finance committee. In this seminar, Hon. Iddi Simba, MP and Chairman of CTI, presented a paper titled 'The Role of Our Industries in a Free Trade Environment' on 16 February, 1996, With the help of Professor Wangwe of ESRF, the Tanzania Chamber of Commerce, Industry and Agriculture prepared a position paper titled 'The Balance of Economic Power in Tanzania.' This paper was also made available to members of parliament. These organised groups believe that they can influence parliament by way of such position papers.

It may be pointed out that all the 27 organised groups that agreed to take part in this study said they did not have any section within their organisations, which specialises in parliamentary affairs. Nor did they have any specific individual assigned the responsibility of dealing with parliament. Most of these organisations handle their affairs with parliament through their legal affairs department.

Position of members of parliament

In order to ascertain the position of members of parliament on lobbying in Tanzania, a number of MP's from both the ruling party and the opposition were consulted.

When asked whether the current parliamentary standing orders allow any form of lobbying to take place, members of parliament responded that currently the standing orders are silent on the issues of lobbying. Members of parliament, however, agree that unofficial lobbying of parliament takes place. A number of unofficial lobbying processes such as literature distribution, personal lobbying, letter writing and committee hearings were cited.

Literature distribution

According to members of parliament, most organised groups unofficially lobby parliament by distributing some literature to members of parliament when in parliament. This literature aims at convincing individual members of Parliament to support or oppose a certain bill. MPs cite some University of Dar es Salaam Faculty of Law members distributed literature regarding the land bill. This literature had a great impact on individual backbench members of parliament, who contributed to the debate from the floor. Those members of parliament who were consulted were of the opinion that the distribution of literature by organised groups should be formalised to avoid government accusations that such groups have sinister motives.

The government sees such literature as subversive because it often takes a position which is contrary to that of the government. Yet, it has to be realised that citizens have a constitutional right to air their views on any legislation that is going to affect their welfare. Furthermore, it is part of the democratisation process and the government should consider it so. Parliament can help the government by formalising the process. This can be done by introducing procedures for inviting experts both from the academic community as well as from all those directly affected by the legislation.

The MP respondents confirmed that currently members of parliament are unable to make meaningful consultations that can help them make better contributions during debates. Two questions were asked to verify this assertion. The first question was: 'How often do you solicit expert information from organisations likely to be affected by pending legislation?' The second question was: 'How often do you solicit opinion regarding a certain bill from relevant organisations?'

The responses to these two questions were similar. All MP respondents said consultation would help. However, they were also unanimous that they have no time to consult and solicit expert information or opinion because bills are often presented to them during sittings. This is contrary to the spirit of three readings and the standing orders that demand that MPs receive bills at least three weeks (21 days) before the first reading in parliament. MPs were unhappy with the way the government presents bills to them in 'ambush form' because it denies them the opportunity to solicit expert opinion and information. This has often led MPs to dwell on peripheral rather than substantive issues because they are less informed on most bills. It is difficult for less informed MPs to counter the government position which is most of the time backed by elite teams of well articulated subject matter experts. Since parliament lacks its own experts, it can solicit written literature from academics as well as from all those who are likely to affected by the proposed legislation.

Written literature that analyses the pros and cons of the proposed legislation would enable parliament to pass legislation that is more beneficial to society. Furthermore, consultations would also allow parliament to better fulfil its constitutional responsibility of supervising the government. Consultations can be made by individual members or by committees.

A clause may be added to the parliamentary standing orders which makes it compulsory for committees to seek written and/or verbal opinion from all those who are likely to be affected by pending legislation in parliament. Those who volunteer literature that analyses the efficacy or weaknesses of the proposed legislation should be encouraged, too. Such literature should be forwarded directly to the relevant committee or to the secretariat for onward transmission to the committee as one of the inputs to be considered in its deliberations.

Personal lobbying

MPs also confirm that personal lobbying is common in Tanzania. Individuals frequent parliament premises to seek audience with individual members of parliament. Many organised groups also send their emissaries to meet a targeted member of parliament, either in Dodoma during Bunge sessions or to their offices in their respective constituencies.

Apart from visits to parliament premises, organised groups as well as other individuals organise pre-arranged meetings in which they try to convince a member of parliament to support a beneficial bill or oppose a bill which appears to undermine the interest of their members. MPs accept the fact that pre-arranged meetings with organised groups are quite effective. Such meetings tend to equip members of parliament with technical information and facts that they use as ammunition during debates. This lobbying is helpful where the issue under discussion does not warrant the application of the three-line whip where members of parliament are compelled to vote with their party.

During the 1996/97 Budget session, some employees of Air Tanzania went to parliament to lobby MPs to support them in their fight against what they perceived to be the Minister of Communication's support of their business rival, Alliance Air Lines. Air Tanzania employees wanted parliament to intervene and reverse the agreement between the ATC Board and Alliance, which enabled Alliance to use ATC's routes. MPs respondents said this lobby failed because of ATC's known inability to fulfill its responsibility to its clients, both locally and internationally.

In the 1996/97-budget session, the Association of Tanzania Oil Manufacturers successfully lobbied the Minister for Finance to give them a tax rebate on imported crude oil. Members of parliament were not however, convinced on the political expediency of this government decision. Therefore, the Minister for Finance 'acting under severe pressure from Members of Parliament decided to revoke his decision to allow importers of crude edible oil to enjoy customs duty and sales tax tariffs which prevailed prior to the 1996/97 Budget (Daily News 26 August 1996).

MPs respondents suggest that personal lobbying of individual members of parliament by organised groups is the most common form of lobbying parliament in Tanzania. This form of lobbying takes place both within and outside the premises of parliament. Representatives of organised groups often visit the parliament when it is in session and talk to individual members of parliament during tea and lunch breaks. However, just like in the case of literature distributed by organised groups, MPs suggest that the government is not particularly happy with this kind of lobbying.

Members of parliament genuinely believe that the Tanzanian government is opposed to lobbying by organised groups. In the words of one MP, 'the government sees organized groups as anti-government, and is suspicious of Members of Parliament who talks to the representatives of organized groups within the premises of parliament.' Backbench members of parliament who talk to representatives of organised groups are often considered to be a disgrace to their party and the government. They are also considered as sellouts. Representatives of organised groups are perceived by the government as subversives whose intention is to brew mischief and to corrupt MPs. This unfortunate misconception of the role of organised groups in seeking to influence parliament has forced many MPs to shy away from openly courting organised groups.

Because organised groups fail to hold formal official talks with members of parliament, they invite them to evening parties for informal talks. Some MPs are not happy with this kind of arrangement because it can lead to unethical lobbying and would prefer the parliamentary standing orders to specify on how organised groups can formally lobby parliament.

The multiparty parliament has tried to formalise some kind of lobbying by organising workshops where they invite experts and academics to give position papers. For example, in May 1996, the Finance and Economic Affairs Committee held a three-day workshop.

The theme of the workshop was 'Strategies and mechanisms for the development of a fast growing and more vibrant integrated economy.' The workshop held in collaboration with the support of the Friedrich Ebert Stiftung Foundation (FES) invited the Executive Director of the Economics and Social Research Foundation as well as the head of the Economics Department of the University of Dar es Salaam to give position papers (See *Bunge News, Toleo la*, 1 April 1996). In April 1996, the Constitutional and Legal Affairs Committee also organised a workshop and invited University of Dar es Salaam experts. This kind of formal lobbying is important, but insufficient to enable the Tanzanian parliament to make better informed policy decisions and more relevant laws. An amendment in the parliamentary standing orders which recognises the imperative need for committees to consult those likely to be affected by the proposed legislation would formalise lobbying.

Members of parliament cited a number of constraints to official lobbying in Tanzania. They said that apart from the silence of parliamentary standing orders on lobbying there are other institutional constraints. One such constraint is the predominant position of the political party over the individual member of parliament. Answers to five different sets of questions have led us to this conclusion.

In the first instance, MPs were asked to rank factors which influences their voting decisions in parliament. The question asked: 'Whenever an MP must decide how he/she will vote on an issue or a bill, he must take several factors into account, such as: the wishes of people in his/her constituency, the views of interest groups, the recommendation of his colleagues and friends, his personal feelings, and the wishes of his political party. In your opinion, which of these kinds of factors are likely to influence your decisions?'

All MP respondents agree that their political party influences them first. The three-line whip is cited as the main reason for voting according to the wishes of the party. Only on rare occasions does an MP vote according to his own conscience.

Apart from the wishes of the political party, most MPs said constituency views are also important to a keen parliamentarian. Nevertheless, most MPs were unanimous that compared to political parties constituents are not well organised and their wishes are not well articulated. Furthermore, since the government does not give MPs bills on time, it is almost impossible for them to solicit the views of their constituencies.

An MP's former profession and officemates appear to have an impact on an MP's decision. This was confirmed by the responses to the following questions: "Does your former profession make you loyal to your former colleagues? Does this influence your voting behavior in parliament?' MPs said they listened to their former colleagues. They also said that they were sympathetic to the predicaments of their former colleagues, to the extent that their debate contributions reflect their sympathy. However, voting as stated earlier is a different story. Voting reflects the wishes of the political party rather than that of the individual MP. Also, the fact that most of the time voting is by acclamation, i.e., by weight of voice rather than by individual roll calls, makes it difficult to determine the voting pattern of individual MPs. Nevertheless, the party three-line whip is often said to be at the back ground when ever an MP votes in parliament.

MPs were also asked two additional questions that reinforced the above answers. They were asked: 'How would you vote for a bill in Parliament if you know that someone is watching?' 'Can you vote for an issue against someone who is watching (party whip)?' MPs were adamant that a keen parliamentarian would have to vote first as the party directs, since it is the party that sponsors him/her to parliament. However, if the party has not directed them otherwise, they would listen to their own conscience. Yet, it is imperative to point out that when asked: 'What organisation has influenced you the most in your decision to support or oppose a motion in parliament?' The MPs replied unanimously, 'my political party.' The influence of the political party in the decision making process in parliament cannot, therefore, be overstated.

The dominant position of the political party in the legislative process appears to be a hindrance to effective lobbying and is a handicap to the effectiveness of a multiparty parliament in supervising the government. Under conditions where the government often threatens MPs of the ruling party with the three-line whip whenever they show independence in debating government bills, parliament becomes ineffective in supervising the conduct of government. This condition is exacerbated by the numerical weakness of the opposition in parliament. Furthermore, the opposition is made even weaker by the mere fact that the shadow cabinet (which is given the first opportunity to debate government bills after the committee chair has responded to the government position) is itself dominated by MPs mostly from one part of the Union, Zanzibar, Pemba and therefore hardly knows the mainland. Such circumstances enable the executive branch of government to dominate the legislative branch of government contrary to the spirit of the constitution.

Prudent application of the three-line whip, i.e., its use for only those matters which are absolutely critical for the survival of the party, will lessen the current too dominant position of the party which reinforces single party mentality in a multiparty parliament.

Letters

Letters to the editor of newspapers also provide another opportunity to lobby parliament. Most of the MPs consulted said they often pay some attention to letters written in newspapers especially where those letters address issues relevant to their constituencies. Furthermore, Tanzanian MPs can also be influenced by letters to the editor particularly those which attack their position or those which pinpoint weaknesses of the government system.

When MPs were asked: 'Do you pay any attention to letters to the editor regarding Members of Parliament and their positions on certain issues?' they unanimously replied that they pay attention not only to letters to the editor but also to newspaper editorials, radio and television commentaries, especially during parliamentary sessions.

It was also observed that it was difficult for rural constituency MPs to pay sustained attention to newspaper letters because they do not regularly have access to newspapers in their constituencies. Yet, they admit that newspapers raise issues that help to bolster their position in parliament. Neverthess, only few debates can be influenced by the mass media. Ultimately, MPs has to vote according to the wishes of their political party.

MPs have also observed that writing letters to the editor as a form of lobbying is ultimately limited by the fact that newspapers, particularly English media news papers which tend to be more analytical and critical are very expensive Most MPs are unable to buy newspapers all the time. Furthermore, the parliamentary library is not up to date on newspapers. MPs also complain that library hours are or not convenient because it is open only during the day when parliament is in session. The library is not open on Saturdays and Sundays when MPs are free.

MPs have also confirmed that they occasionally receive letters from their constituencies urging them to take certain positions. However, the letters they receive are few and sporadic and not well articulated. However, MPs would receive many more letters originating from their constituencies raising substantive issues would raise the quality of debate in parliament and strengthen constituency representation. It should be pointed out that, like many other forms of lobbying in Tanzania, letter writing has little influence on the legislative process. This is because of the voting behaviour of the current parliament is most of the time determined by party officials rather than individual conscience of the member of parliament.

Committee hearings

Committee hearings also provide a limited opportunity for lobbying parliament in Tanzania. Committee hearings assume that each relevant committee will have enough time and resources to cater for invited experts whenever a government bill is presented to the committee. Most important is to seek opinions of those who are likely to be affected by the pending legislation.

Occasionally different parliamentary committees invite expert opinion. The Finance and Economic Affairs Committee invited the Chambers of Commerce to express their opinion on the 1996/97 Government Budget Recommendations. The Committee on Parliamentary Privileges and Services to Members used 'The 1988 Parliamentary Immunities, Powers and Privileges act,' to invite different experts from the National Insurance Corporation, Parastatal Pension Fund, the Treasury, and the Ministry of Health when it was preparing its April 1996 report. Such consultations provide an excellent opportunities for lobbying to take place.

However, when MPs were asked how good the legislative process in Tanzania is, they all agreed that the legislative process as it is on paper is very good. Yet, they were also quick to point out that 'practice prohibit the well functioning of the legislative process'. For one thing, the government does not make an effort to ensure that MPs receive bills on time. Bills rarely reach the constituency in time to solicit views that can help an MP to contribute meaningfully in parliamentary debates. Some MPs cited the fact that more often than not, the submission of bills does not table to the Constitutional and Legal Affairs Committee whose task is to ensure that it does not contravene the constitution.

Secondly, the mandate of the standing committees is limited. When MPs were asked 'In your opinion, how effective are legislative committees in enhancing the legislative process in Tanzania?' 'Do these committees help to sustain a proper legislative process in Tanzania?' 'Do committees provide an opportunity for lobbying parliament? they replied that section 69, (2), of the Parliamentary Standing Orders does not empower committees to make changes to any government bill. This means that committees can only deliberate and make recommendations that the government can accept or ignore. Parliamentary standing committees should be given mandate to reject government bills if they strongly feel that these bills were hastily prepared. Such powers will not only compel the government to present to parliament better prepared bills, but will also enhance the status of parliament. Parliament will be seen to be able to supervise the government in accordance with in the constitution.

MPs are also of the opinion that committees are unable to make much impact on government bills because the government has a monopoly of information and expertise. Indeed, the lack research assistants handicaps, most MPs from debating issues and making decisions based on accurate information. The government has an edge over parliament on this score. Lobbying, if formalised, would arrest this situation.

Furthermore, the standing orders do not allow committees to call resource persons or experts in the relevant field other than government civil servants or parastatal employees. On those few occasions, when the committees invite such experts, they tend to become government accomplices, and defend the government. This is cited as a limitation to official lobbying of parliament in Tanzania. Committees should be given the mandate to invite any resource persons to assist them with expertise and information that will enable the committees to make a thorough analysis of government bills.

As already mentioned, perhaps the most serious limitation is the short time that committees are given to discuss government bills. MPs complained that sometimes committee members are recalled from plenary sessions to discuss a government bill that has just been submitted. This means that committee members are denied the opportunity to participate in the plenary sessions. The absence of committee members in debating bills during plenary sessions due to committee assignments undermines their democratic right to air their views. Furthermore, they are not given adequate time to study the bills. Nor are committees given enough time to make adequate consultations with experts within and outside parliament. MPs blame the government's lack of a legislative calendar for the fire brigade approach to government legislation in parliament. Bills are presented under a certificate of urgency, a trick often used to deny committee members enough time to make consultations that can enable them to analyse government bills thoroughly.

It is in the course of intensive consultations during committee hearings that recommendations are elaborated for presentation to the plenary sessions of the whole parliament. One is tempted to recommend adoption of procedures used elsewhere which ensures a more effective and democratic legislative process. In the German *Bundesrat*, for example, according to *Fischer(date:30)* 'The committees must have completed their consultations two weeks prior to the plenary session. The recommendations of the individual committees are compiled and printed by the office of the committee responsible. The printed recommendations form the basis for the rest of the decision-making process' in parliament.

When discussing The Loans and Advances Realisation Trust (Amendments) Bill, 1996, Hon. Juma J. Akukweti, the chairman of the Finance and Economic Affairs Committee complained that the government deliberately denied them the opportunity to research and make expert consultations which rendered them ineffective to make worthwhile recommendations. He complained further that the committee lacked power to reject a government bill, therefore, the government did not give his committee enough time to discuss the

1996 LART Bill. Indeed the committee had refused to discuss the bill and asked for more time at least a month, in order to give the committee enough time to make a thorough analysis and advise the House and the government accordingly (Hansard, 18 April:1996:90-91). The government ignored committee recommendations and presented the bill to the full plenary of parliament. It is imperative to point out that the bill was discussed and passed by the plenary of the House despite an impassioned plea from the committee chair. The government's ability to bulldoze standing committees and hoodwink the whole assembly into accepting its position undermines parliament's constitutional responsibility to supervise the government. The government's power to ignore committee recommendations wholesale renders them ineffective. The whole legislative process is undermined. Checks and balances between the two branches have to be introduced, if the prestige of parliament is to be restored. Mechanisms have to be worked out such that the different branches can counter each other. The committee stage is a proper place to start.

Empowering standing committees power to reject a government bill if proper procedures of the legislative process are not followed can rectify such an anomaly. The procedures demand that there must be enough time between the first and the second readings of a bill to give committee members enough time to make intensive consultations. This is not currently the case as amplified by the 1996 LART Bill, which committee members thought was not urgent enough to deny them time to study and analyse it. Furthermore, there must be enough time for MPs to read the committee recommendations before they start plenary sessions on a government bill.

Patronage

MPs are prominent members of Tanzanian society. Some MPs are chairmen of public corporations; some are board members of both public and private enterprises, while others are district or regional heads of government. Other members of parliament are prominent businessmen and women and members of chambers of commerce etc. This has made MPs a target for lobbying. MPs consulted suggest that organised groups invite them to unofficial social functions and use the privilege of informal gatherings to lobby them. MPs are also often invited to address members of organised groups where they use the occasion to lobby government. It was for example reported in the *Daily News* of 10 April 1996 that, 'The Government has been urged to speed up the creation of an atmosphere that will encourage the growth of a private sector willing to invest more and pay appropriate taxes.' This message was given by the chairman of the Confederation of Tanzania Industries (CTI), Mr Iddi Simba, who also spoke as member of parliament for Ilala, when he was addressing members of the Dar es Salaam North Rotary Club, District 9210. This is a simple example of how organised groups lobby individual members of parliament. Furthermore, as members of organised groups they get lobbied within the offices of their respective organisations.

Procedural changes

This study shows that organised groups do lobby parliament in Tanzania. However, most of the lobbying is not systematic since no institutionalised form of lobbying structure exists. The main complaint is that parliament passes legislation which affects members of organised groups without consulting them. Organised groups would like parliament to be compelled to consult them before passing any legislation that is likely to affect their members.

The study reveals that most organised groups lobby members of parliament in their individual capacity. Consultations with organised groups indicate that only sympathetic members of parliament are lobbied. Furthermore, some organised groups try to lobby parliament by holding seminars and inviting members of parliament to attend. Still others prepare position papers and submit them to members of parliament.

Consultations with some members of parliament appear to corroborate observations from organised groups. While MPs are of the opinion that current legislative procedures provide little room for official lobbying, they nevertheless agree that most lobbying of parliament in Tanzania is informal. This informal lobbying takes the form of literature distribution, personal lobbying and letters to the newspaper editors and to individual members of parliament and even patronage. Under patronage, an MP, who also happens to be the boss of some organised groups takes the opportunity to lobby the executive branch of government on behalf of his group. Such an MP may also lobby parliament on behalf of members of his organisation. Patronage lobbying is, however, restricted by parliamentary standing orders and procedures that require an MP to declare his/her interest before discussing a bill in which he/she has vested interests. There have also been few instances where the various standing committees have consulted various organised groups such as institutions of higher learning.

Need for procedural changes

What procedural and legal changes should be made to overcome existing constraints that inhibit parliament from articulating with the wider society in Tanzania? Articulating with the wider society assumes that parliamentary procedures enhance parliamentary lobbying rather than inhibit it. This means that procedures should allow organised groups as well as other members of society to have access to parliament, and to make contributions that may enable parliament to make better informed decisions. One effective way of accessing parliament is during committee hearings. This calls for the following pre-conditions.

Committee consultations

Currently parliamentary standing orders are not clear on lobbying. They need to be made clearer. The Parliamentary Immunities, Powers and Privileges Act, 1988 (No.3 of 1988) empowers any standing committee of parliament to 'order any person to attend it and to give evidence – or to produce any document in the possession of, or under the control of such person.' Such powers are granted to the committees only when a parliamentary inquiry is in progress. However, standing orders are silent when it comes to committee deliberations of a government bill.

The standing committee analysing a government bill should make as many consultations as possible to get as much information as possible. Such consultations should be made before a committee reaches a decision on any bill under its jurisdiction. Intensive consultations will enable standing committees to make elaborate recommendations for presentation to the full plenary of parliament and to offer better advice to parliament and the government on the adequacy of the proposed legislation. Furthermore, the formalisation of official lobbying will ensure the image of parliament is not tarnished by the possible abuses of unofficial lobbying. Official lobbying will eliminate or at least minimise under-the-table dealings so prevalent under unofficial lobbying.

There is need to amend section 69 of the Parliamentary Standing Orders to be read in conjunction with Act No. 3/88 on Parliamentary Privileges. Act 3/88 does not enable the public to air their views on a bill. It, however, enables a standing committee to call for evidence in a parliamentary inquiry. This amendment should therefore make it clearer that standing committees should call for expert information, advice and opinion on a bill. Calling for information and advice should be more formalised to enable citizens to take part in the legislative process and should enable standing committees to offer better advice to parliament and the government on the adequacy of the proposed legislation.

Committee powers to amend or reject bills

When a bill is presented in parliament the committee discuses it as per Parliamentary Standing Orders, section 69, (1). However, it is also imperative to point out that section 69, (2), of these standing orders prohibit committees from changing a government bill. Only the government has powers to make amendments. Such an arrangement gives the government more powers over the legislative process than parliament itself. This is contrary to the spirit of section 63, (2), of the Constitution of the United Republic of Tanzania, which gives parliament supreme powers to supervise and advise the government. Moreover, it encourages the government to present hastily prepared bills because it is aware that current legislative procedures provide enough loopholes to force its way, even when a standing committee is opposed, as was the case with the LART bill mentioned earlier. The credibility of parliament as well as that of the government suffers immensely.

It is therefore recommended that a parliamentary standing committee should be given enough powers to amend and, if need be, reject a government bill which, after thorough consultation and analysis, is not worth recommending to the full plenary. Such powers will not only enhance the status of parliament but will also compel the government to prepare better bills. Furthermore, if committees are given powers to amend or reject a government bill before it is discussed in the plenary it would help to sustain a proper legislative process and enable parliament to make more effective laws. This will save parliament from wasting time on ill-prepared bills.

Committees to have access to expert information

There is need for standing committees to have access to expert information on subjects before committees. This can be fulfilled through secretariat briefs. The parliamentary secretariat should carry out research on the implications of bills and prepare briefs that can enable standing committee to have a better grasp of the issues pertaining to a bill. In addition to secretariat briefs, standing committees should call evidence from relevant quarters as well. Committees should also call witnesses should the need arise.

Need for adequate time for committee consultations

The three readings system was introduced in order to give committees more time to scrutinise government bills. However, as mentioned earlier, MPs complain that they are not given enough time to make consultations. There is also need for committees to have more time to study issues before it. It is therefore, further recommended that committees should be made to complete their consultations at least two weeks prior to the plenary session. This will enable committees to interview and receive evidence that will enable the committee to reach proper decisions and make recommendations to the full plenary of parliament. Adequate time will give MPs ample time to prepare for plenary debates. This will enable parliament to make better laws. Parliamentary procedures requiring three readings and time between the readings should be respected.

Need to avail committee recommendations to other MPs

Furthermore, committee recommendations about a government bill should be compiled, printed and made available to other MPs. In addition, the printed committee recommendations should form the basis for the rest of the legislative decision making process in parliament.

Need for a clear legislative programme
Government should have a legislative programme. Effective lobbying requires that information should reach people within ample time. Therefore the government should allow people's interests to guide its policy formulation. The will of the people should be the will of the government. Indeed, a government's legislative programme is a prerequisite for any meaningful lobbying of parliament.

Bills should be widely publicised
Bills should be widely publicised via newspapers, radio and television to enable citizens to respond and make contributions that will enable parliament to make more workable laws.

Need to revise certificate of urgency in legislation
The certificate of urgency in legislation needs to be revisited. A more cautious and prudent use of the certificate of urgency in passing legislation in parliament is necessary. It is therefore recommended that members of a standing committee should make a recommendation on the adequacy of using such a certificate. Members of parliament should be able to vote in a plenary on whether an issue deserves to be presented under certificate of urgency following committee recommendations. Parliament should introduce a clause in the standing orders that any bill that does not meet the 21 days requirement for three readings should not be allowed by the relevant standing committee.

All the above recommendations involve only procedural changes and not legal changes. Therefore, these changes, which only involve rules for executing its responsibilities can be quickly effected by parliament. Although the changes are not substantive, their implementation would improve the legislative process in Tanzania by making parliament more accessible than is currently the case.

References

Ball, A.R. (1971). *Modern Politics and Government*, London MacMillan.
Budgen, N. (1966). *Myth of the Lobbjist*, The House Magazine.
Burrell, M. (1996). *Backstage Bores*, The House Magazine.

Fischer, L. (2nd ed). *The German Bundestrat: The Second Legislative Body*, Bonn: The Bundestrat, Public Relations Office.
Ford, G. (1966). *Lobbying: Travelling with Phanthoms*, The House Magazine.
Hague, R., et al. (3rd ed) (1992). *Comparative Government and Politics: An Introduction*, London: MacMillan.
Jamhuri ya Muungano wa Tanzania (1995a). *Katiba ya Jamhuri ya Muungano wa Tanzania ya Mwaka 1977*. Dar es Salaam: Mpiga Chapa wa Serikali.
Jamhuri ya Muungano wa Tanzania. (1995b). *Bunge la Tanzania: Kanuni za Bunge*. Dar es Salaam: Mpiga Chapa wa Serikali.
Jamhuri ya Muungano wa Tanania (1996). *Bunge la Tanzania: Taarifa ya Kamati ya Haki na Huduma za Bunge*, Dodoma.
Jones, B. and Kavanagh, D. (4th ed) (1990). *British Politics today*, Manchester: Manchester University Press.
Kingdom, J. (1991). *Government and Politics in Britain: An Introduction*. London, MacMillan.
Mendalsohn, L. (1996). *Question of Ethics*, The House Magazine.
Milbrath, L.W. (1970). '*Lobbyists Approach Government*' in Robert, H. Salisbury, *Interest Group Politics in Africa*. New Year: Harper & Row.
Moran, M. (2nd ed) (1991). *Politics and Society in Britain: An Introduction*, London: MacMillan.
Msekwa, P. (1995). *Essays on the Transition to Multipartism in Tanzania*, Dar es Salaam: DUP.
Peak, G.W. and Zeiglar, L.H. (1972). *Interest Groups in American Society*, Englewood: Prentice Hall Inc.
Punnet, R.M. (6th ed) (1994). *British Government and Politics*. Dartmouth.
Raj, H. (1990). *Comperative Politics*, New Delhi: Subject Politications.
Salisbury, R.H. (1970). *Interest Group Politics in America*, New York: Harper & Row.
Stewart, J.D. (1958). *British Pressure Groups: Their Roles in Relation to the House of Commons*, Oxford: OUP.
Thompson, L. (1996). *Influence with Honour*, The House Magazine.

9

The Political Competence of Voters and their Members of Parliament

Amos Mhina

Introduction

While the evaluation of the political competence of a member of parliament (MP) can come at any time of the term of office, citizens usually express their views on the matter during election time. Voters evaluate candidates before elections. This means that voters only have an opportunity to pass judgement on the performance of a seating MP or the potential of a candidate seeking to enter parliament for the first time only during election time. During the single party rule, screening done by the ruling party limited and influenced the choice of electors on the competence of candidates. Even more limiting, however, was the fact that the electorate had no say on the considerable number of MPs selected indirectly to join the parliament. In 1985, for example, out of 244 MPs, the number elected from the constituencies was 165 and out of these 50 came from the islands of Zanzibar. (Mhina, 1993).

In this era of multiparty politics, the possibility of citizens choosing competent leaders is partly reduced by party choices, which are becoming more and more dominated by money. The candidates presented to voters are sometimes those who have passed through controversial primaries and not always the best candidates. Once the MPs are elected, the voters have to wait for the next elections to change their representatives even if they prove to be incompetent long before the end of their terms.

The chapter analyses views on the political competence of an MP from the perspective of voters and parliamentarians. The questions solicited voter respondents' views on three issues. The first sought views on the power to deal with an under performing MP in the constituencies. The second sought opinion on the desirability of instituting a mechanism for removing an incompetent MP. Thirdly, the respondents were asked to express views as to which possible institutions should be deciding on these important national matters.

Other questions were posed to MPs. These questions sought their views on the possibility of voters being able to discipline and even remove an incumbent MP whom they considered to have poor job performance. Other questions tried to establish the MPs views on their office environment and whether such environment allowed them to carry out their national and constituency duties properly. MPs were also asked their opinion on possible mechanisms to be instituted for removing an incompetent MP.

The role of a member of parliament in Tanzania

It is important to establish at the onset the role of an MP in the Tanzanian setting so as to establish the context for analysis of the responses.

MPs in Tanzania are representatives of citizens in the National Assembly. This body has four main functions; to pass laws, to vote for taxation so as to provide the means of carrying out the work of government, to scrutinise government policy and administration, including proposal for expenditure and to debate the major issues of the day (Bungetz.org 1998). This unicameral parliament in Tanzania is dominated by constituency MPs. The exceptions include women MPs picked from party lists based on proportional representation to make up 20 per cent of the National Assembly. Other non-constituency MPs are five selected from the Zanzibar House of Representatives, and the ex-official attorney general. There are also 10 MPs appointed by the president. The three categories are not accountable to any clear citizen constituencies. The women MPs are accountable first and foremost to their political parties and it is hard to justify the five members from the Zanzibar House. At the same time, the presidential appointments, which were absent in 1995, made a come back in 2000 and they can be used to good effect when election results are quite close.

The tasks of an MP are seen at three levels: the national level, the constituency and the local level. At the national level, the MP is responsible for making of laws, amending the constitution, passing of the budget and other financial laws. They also contribute to national policies and strategies, oversee government action, participate in the allocation and mobilisation of national resources, linking the government and his/her constituency and provide national leadership. To carry out these tasks, the MP can be a member of committees both inside and outside the House or a board member of public organisations.

At the constituency level, the MP is responsible for facilitating the implementation of government policies and decisions. The MP is expected to be part of the process of securing various constituency problems. The MP is also expected to relay the needs of the constituency to the government for appropriate action. At the same time he/she is expected to mobilise resources and people for development activities and generally provide leadership in the constituency.

There has been controversy concerning the roles of MPs from the opposition parties. The legacy of one party rule still lingers for the ruling party and top government leaders, on one hand and leaders of opposition parties, on the other. Since CCM has continued to be in power, its leaders have, at times, threatened to cut or withdraw development funds from constituencies that elect candidates belonging to opposition parties! At the same time, some opposition party officials have not taken kindly to their MPs who collaborate with CCM leaders in useful development projects of their constituencies. Some have been criticised for joining the president's or prime minister's delegation making developmental tours of opposition MPs' constituencies.

The two reactions show lack of maturity in the multiparty culture of Tanzania. In plural politics a country is directed by the programme of the party which has won the last election. The party and its cadres are however, not expected to be involved in the day to day administration of the programme. Nor is it justified to expect civil servants, who after all are barred from being members of political parties, to behave like party cadres. Likewise, it cannot be justified for a national leader to threaten to deprive taxpayers of development funds for exercising their constitutional right to elect a leader of their choice. It would seem to us that the Chama Cha Mapinduzi (CCM) is yet to make the transition from a vanguard party to an electoral party. The party need not disappear during the years between elections as is the case with some parties in the West, yet it seems quite inappropriate to threaten civil servants in the day to day running of government.

In the same vein, it has not sank in the minds of some opposition party leaders and their members that the citizens are sovereign and do not exist as a privilege of political parties, but it is the reverse which is true. An elected MP has the responsibility first and foremost to the people of his constituency and only secondly to his party. It is unjustified for party leader, with no reasons of principle, to prevent an MP from participating in the activities of his constituency. The above reasons and others justify posing the question of sanctioning an incumbent MP before his or her term is over. Five years of MP inaction is costly to a constituency.

At the local and inter-personal level, the MP is a politician and his image very much depends on how he publicises himself and the nature of his actions – making him popular and showing his achievement as well as other issues that give MPs a national stature. The performance of MPs with respect to these tasks varies. Unfortunately, in the absence of viable development programmes in the constituencies, many citizens judge the performance of their MPs at this interpersonal level, where symbolic public relation gestures can have an impact.

For some MPs who do not have constituencies in the administrative sense, for example, appointed MPs and those holding the special women seats, it is difficult to evaluate performance. Due to the nature of their appointment, allegiance to party leaders is expected to be stronger than to an undefined constituency. The setting aside of women seats is important in the light of systematic gender segregation which still has its roots in the country. However, these women should know that they represent the women constituency and not their parties. There is need for a mechanism to make women MPs accountable to all Tanzanian women, and not just to *Umoja wa Wanawake Tanzania* (UWT) of CCM or other party caucuses. Constituencies, could be created either at administrative district or regional level in order to allow competition. Another alternative would be to establish an elaborate system, applicable to all parties, for the selection of women MPs.

From the side of MPs it has been observed that there is disparity between the expected role of the MP and actual performance in the context of the Tanzania government and politics. The disparity is observed at the level of resources available to MPs, but also by the political and administrative culture, which has developed over the years, mostly dominated by single party rule. (Ngotolainyo 1997).

A poor nation, like Tanzania, finds it difficult to adequately provide resources both for the administration of the National Assembly and for the MPs. While MPs feel that they are not adequately provided for, average Tanzanians feel that the MPs are overpaid, especially when compared to ordinary civil servants. With 250 MPs, the size of National Assembly is considerable, the geographical size of the country notwithstanding. This is compounded by the fact that the conditionality of Union makes Zanzibar over-represented in the National Assembly. It is unlikely that the MPs will vote to reduce their numbers. What could be done is to stop the increase of constituencies and the number of appointed MPs. In order for MPs to be well provided for so as to fulfil their duties adequately, their numbers should be manageable given the size of the economy.

At present, MPs demand assistants and adequate offices. The question of offices is more critical for opposition MPs because most of the MPs offices in the constituencies are located in CCM buildings (Ngotolainyo, 1997). It is evident, therefore, that the political culture of single party rule still has an influence, even on the administrative performance of the National Assembly. It would appear there is no sense of urgency to ensure the availability of such facilities.

Certainly, the roles of an MP from the ruling party and that of his/her opposition counterpart are bound to differ, especially in a system influenced by the Westminster model, as is the case with most Commonwealth parliaments. Writing about the House of Representatives of Zanzibar, Silima (1997) highlights some of the differences, which are similar to the Union parliament. After noting that an MP is responsible to his/her party, which gives him/her a ticket on which to contest, he outlines the roles of an MP of the ruling party. These include the supervision of the implementation of his/her party programme, facilitating the passage of the government budget, ensuring the adoption of government bills, ensuring that all levels of government are performing their duties adequately and to support all decisions made by the government. The role of an opposition party MP, in his opinion, is to assist the government of the day to implement its activities well. Such MPs are also supposed to make corrections and propose amendments to government bills and budget estimates, to oversee the use of public revenue and lastly to criticise, correct and where due, congratulate the government on its performance.

The above are valid distinctions, although the independent role of MPs of either camps does not come out clearly vis-a-vis party control and in relation to representing the citizens of his constituency. Up to now the relationship between MPs of the two camps has been far from the ideal as mentioned by Silima. Often it has been acrimonious. The size of the CCM majority has often led it to ignore the small number of opposition MPs. Such conflicts are indeed normal in all pluralist parliaments, the distinction between them is when the two camps act as if they are irreconcilable enemies.

Both camps need to change their attitudes, especially as the role of the National Assembly (NA) is likely to expand through revitalisation of NA committees, some of them chaired by members of the opposition. Such collaboration is likely to enhance the work and respect of the committees. The Public Accounts Committee (PAC) is a good example. Since the office of the accountant general and that of controller and auditor general have been strengthened as a result of government reforms and good governance, their annual reports play an important place in Tanzania. The auditor general's report is increasingly regarded as important, and it is presented to the PAC which can summon accounting officers and discipline them, if necessary. The performance of PAC, including summoning top civil servants, is likely to enhance accountability in the utilisation of national resources.

Other committees are also likely to be increasingly important especially because reforms call for more transparency in the performance of leaders and programmes which require parliamentary scrutiny. It is against this background that we examine the responses of voters and MPs on political competence as regards the role of MPs.

Views on the role of members of parliament as representatives of the people

The purpose of having a sample of voters and MPs was to capture the different perceptions of the two groups. The perception of voters is important to establish whether they are aware that they have important decisions to make as regards their representatives.

Views of voters

As indicated in the methodology chapter, respondents were drawn from 12 constituencies, from the Mainland and Zanzibar. One issue of investigation concerned the voters' opinion on what they could do to sanction a poorly performing incumbent MP.

Table 9.1 Voters' capacity to deal with an under performing MP

Response	No. of Respondents	%
1. Can't do anything	206	32.2
2. Unseat before election	41	6.4
3. Can be summoned	87	13.6
4. Can complain to party	19	3
5. Can complain to government	40	6.3
6. No re-election	116	26
7. Others	6	1
8. H/KK	74	11.6
	639	100

Table 9.1 shows that the highest category of respondents (32.2 per cent) believed that they could not do anything to an incumbent MP. The second highest group (26 per cent) believed that what they could do was not to re-elect the MP which meant that their action could only come at the end of his or her term. Those who believe that they could do something before the end of the term make up 29.3 per cent. Out of these, 13.6 per cent believe they could summon the MP and express their dissatisfaction while 9.3 per cent believed they could complain either to the government or to their respective parties. The data through

The Political Competence of Voters

Table 9.2: Voters' capacity to deal with under performing MP - percentages by constituencies

		Arusha	Bukene	Nzega East	Mbeya Urban	Chake Chake	Ziwani	Moshi Rural	Vunjo	Mtwara Rural	Chaani	Bukoba	Nkenge
1.	Can't do anything	30.0	50	32.5	36.3	22.5	35.0	42.5	37.5	30.0	30.0	12.5	30.8
2.	Unseat before election 5.1		7.5	22	2.5	8.8	10.0	2.5	5.0	2.5	1.3	0	17.5
3.	Can be summoned	8.8	12.5	7.5	7.5	20.0	15	10.0	20	10	27	20.0	10.2
4.	Complain to party	1.3	0	2.5	2.5	2.5	10.0	0	2.5	6.3	1.3	5.0	2.6
5.	Complain to govt.	20.0	2.5	0	2.5	0	0	10.0	7.5	2.5	5.0	10.0	10.3
6.	No re-election	26.3	12.5	55	21.3	22.5	12.5	10.0	27.5	38.8	21.3	27.5	33.3
7.	Others	–	–	–	–	–	–	–	–	–	–		
8.	H/KK	6.3	0	0	18.8	22.5	25.0	22.5	0	11.3	13.8	7.5	7.7

cross-tabulation further shows that there are marked differences between constituencies, see (Table 9.2).

Table 9.2 shows that the people of Bukene at 50 per cent score highest in believing that they could not do anything about a poorly performing incumbent MP. Moshi rural follows with 42.5 per cent.

On the question which sought the opinion on the desirability of a proposal to remove mid-term an incompetent MP, we find an overriding majority of respondents in agreement with the proposal, see (Table 9.3).

Table 9.3: Views on a possible proposal to remove an incompetent incumbent MP

Response	Respondents	%
Like/accept proposal	462	72.3
Do not like it	94	14.7
It depends	17	2.7
Others	30	4.7
H/KK	36	5.6
	639	100

Only 14.7 per cent of the respondents did not like the idea. This means that the majority of voters would like to sanction incumbents in the case of poor performance before their term is over. Again, there are differences among the constituencies on this issue. A number of constituencies are above the 72.3 per cent national average. The constituencies which are in agreement with the proposal at more than 80 per cent are Arusha, Nzega East, Vunjo and Chaani. This is shown in Table 9.4.

Table 9.4: Views on proposal to remove incompetent incumbent MP - by constituencies

		Arusha	Bukene	Nzega East	Mbeya Urban	Chake Chake	Ziwani	Moshi Rural	Vunjo	Mtwara Rural	Chaani	Bukoba	Nkenge
1.	Agree	81.3	72.5	80.0	78.8	70.0	70	72.5	85.0	46.3	83.8	67.5	59.0
2.	Disagree	17.5	7.5	2.5	8.8	12.5	12.5	5.0	10.0	40.0	11.3	25.0	5.1
3.	Depends	0	5.0	0	2.5	2.5	0	15.0	0	5.0	1.3	0	2.6
4.	Others	1.3	2.5	5.0	8.8	12.5	17.5	7.5	0	6.3	2.5	0	7.5
5.	H/KK	–	–	–	–	–	–	–	–	–	–	–	–

Table 9.4 shows that only Mtwara Rural with 46.3 per cent has a score of less than 50 per cent on the desirability of sanctioning an incumbent MP before his or her term is over. Even in Mtwara Rural, however, those in favour are still more than the 40 per cent in opposition to such a proposal.

Respondents were also asked their opinions on the institution they thought should have the last say on important national issues. The responses showed that most thought such power should rest with the president and his government.

Table 9.5: Views on the institution to have supreme decision making powers on the issue

	Responses	%
1. Parliament	156	24.4
2. Ruling party	76	11.9
3. Opposition parties	11	1.7
4. President/government	276	43.2
5. Parliament and government	14	2.2
6. Parliament and ruling party	4	.6
7. Parliament and opposition parties	1	.2
8. Govt. and ruling party	15	2.3
9. Ruling party and opposition party	0	0
10. Other combination	6	.9
11. All together	6	.9
12. It depends	57	8.9
13. Others	17	2.7
14. H/KK	0	0
Total	639	100

With 43.2 per cent the presidency and government stands above the others. The National Assembly with 24.4 per cent stands a poor second. This implies that the majority of voter respondents do not consider the parliament as being supreme. Such supremacy would in the final analysis embody the sovereignty of citizens, as parliament would be made of their representatives.

Table 9.6: Views on supreme decision making institution - by constituency

	Arusha	Bukene	Nzega East	Mbeya Urban	Chake Chake	Ziwani	Moshi Rural	Vunjo	Mtwara Rural	Chaani	Bukoba	Nkenge
1. Parliament	35.0	17.5	15.0	50.0	12.5	7.5	10.0	22.5	25.0	10.0	42.5	23.1
2. Ruling party	16.3	10.0	12.5	6.3	12.5	7.5	15.0	30.0	13.8	6.3	7.5	10.3
3. The president/ government	38.8	50.0	45.0	25.0	47.5	37.5	52.5	40.0	40.0	65.0	37.5	43.6

When we look at responses along constituency lines, one finds that only Mbeya Urban and Bukoba respondents thought the parliament should have more power than the presidency. Mbeya respondents with 50 per cent score highest in this category. Bukoba follows with 42.5 per cent.

Table 9.6 shows that in Arusha, Bukene, Nzega, Mtwara, Chaani and Nkenge respondents considered parliament the second most important institution in decision making, while respondents in Moshi Rural and Vunjo put the ruling party in that spot.

Views of the members of parliament

One hundred Members of parliament were asked a number of questions seeking to establish their political capacity and responsibility and the powers of their voters vis-à-vis the representative to the National Assembly. Their opinions on the powers of voters to sanction an incumbent MP indicate the way MPs view the sovereignty of their voters.

Table 9.7: Views on the powers of constituency voters to sanction an incumbent MP

Response	No. of respondents	%
1. Can't do anything	21	21.0
2. Unseat before election	6	6.0
3. Can be summoned	53	53.0
4. Complain to party	7	7.0
5. Complain to government	11	11.0
6. No re-election	1	1.0
7. Others	0	0
8. H/KK	1	1.0
Total	100	100

MPs responses show marked a difference from those of the voters. While the highest category of voters (32.2 per cent) believed that they could not do anything, the majority of MPs (53 per cent) believe that voters can summon an MP. At the same time, 21 per cent of the MPs believe that the voters cannot do anything which is the second most important category. While 26 per cent of the voter respondents believed they could sanction the MP through non-election, only 1 per cent of MPs believed that this would be the appropriate recourse. Most likely, MPs would prefer to be summoned than to be sanctioned through non-election.

Another question asked the respondents their opinions on the adequacy of means and authority available to MPs to enable them to carry out both national and constituency duties.

Table 9.8: Views on means and authority of MPs to carry their constituency duties

Response	Respondents	%
1. Very adequate means	1	1.0
2. Adequate means	11	11.0
3. Inadequate means	50	50
4. No means	3	3.0
5. It depends	6	6.0
6. Others	27	27.0
7. H/KK	2	2.0
Total	100	100

Table 9.8 shows that 50 per cent of MPs believe that there are inadequate means and authority available to them. Only 11 per cent believe they have adequate means. These responses correspond to statements by MPs in workshop and meetings on the inadequacies of the office of the MP in the constituencies, in terms of material facilities and authority *vis-a-vis* other institutions, such as local governments and central government departments. Similar views were expressed concerning their means and authority at the national level.

Table 9.9: Views on means and authority of MPs to carry national duties

Response	Respondents	%
1. Very adequate means	2	2.0
2. Adequate means	16	16.0
3. Inadequate means	43	43.0
4. No means	3	3.0
5. It depends	4	4.0
6. Others	30	30.0
7. H/KK	2	2.0
Total	100	100

Table 9.9 shows that 43 per cent of respondents stated that they have inadequate means, compared to the 50 per cent at constituency level. All the same only 16 per cent of the respondents believe that the means are adequate at this level, again there is only a slight increase from the 11 per cent at the constituency level. The MPs were also asked whether they would support a proposition that there should be a mechanism for removing an incompetent incumbent MP before the end of term.

Table 9.10: Views on a possible proposal to remove an incompetent MP before end of term

Response	Respondents	%
1. Accept/like the idea	31	31.0
2. I do not accept/like	54	54.0
3. It depends	8	8.0
4. Other proposals	6	6.0
5. H/KK	1	1.0
Total	100	100

It is not surprising that most MPs (54 per cent) do not like the idea of removing an incumbent before the end of his or her term, compared to the overwhelming 72.3 per cent of voters who were in favour. Only 14.7 per cent of the voter respondents thought that it was a bad idea.

At the same time, only 31 per cent of MPs believe that it is a good idea, probably because they think they could stand the test of competence. This reflects a degree of different interests between the MPs and their voters. While the MPs support security of position once elected, the voters wish to be able to sanction an MP who is not performing as well as expected.

Conclusion

The Tanzania parliament is influenced by two important factors. The first is the legacy of the single party system. As it happens, CCM has a very comfortable majority in the National Assembly, yet the individual role of even a CCM MP is limited. It takes a courageous CCM MP to assert his individual point of view and withstand the CCM parliamentary committee and other party bodies. MPs from the opposition have complained about lack of offices and lack of cooperation from government leaders. At the same time, party leaders have limited the MPs capacity to provide services to their voters in their constituencies.

It is noteworthy that a good number of MPs believe that their voters can summon them in case of poor performance. They do not agree, however, that it is necessary to monitor the performance of MPs or to sanction them before the end of their term. Voters, on their part, believe there is very little they could do in the present set up to sanction incumbents who are under performing. They, however, think it would be a desirable step to sanction their MPs for poor performance.

The second influence on parliament in Tanzania is the Westminster model. That system functions democratically when the majority in the House is only modest. When the party in power has absolute majority very little can limit the power of the executive. Since CCM has such an overriding majority, it can do what it wishes. It can and has amended the constitution to suit its wishes. Only a successful rebellion of its MPs can threaten the executive. At this juncture, it is unlikely that CCM MPs would pass an amendment to the laws to limit its powers through mid-term sanctions.

Yet the analysis shows that the performance of MPs at national and constituency levels needs to be improved. The call for more transparency and good governance will invariably increase the role of the National Assembly at national level. It has to be facilitated to carry out such duties. It is also true that most MPs have largely failed to facilitate development in their constituencies. It is imperative, therefore, that a new working relationship between MPs and their voters be established.

References

Bungetz.org (2001) interafrica.com

Mhina A.K. (1993). 'Tanzanie: Participation ou controle oligarchique' in Duboscq P. and Quantin P., *Les Paysans du Monde: Electeurs sous influence,* Paris: L'Harmattan.

Ngotolainyo; (1997).'Ubunge', REDET, *Hali ya Kisiasa Tanzania*, July 1997.

Ame S.M (1997). 'Uwakilishi', REDET, *Hali ya Kisiasa Tanzania*, July 1997.

10

Comparing Performances: The 1990-1995 Single-Party Parliament and the 1995-2000 Multi-party Parliament

Bernadeta Killian

Introduction

The area of legislative behaviour and processes is the most unexplored terrain of Tanzanian politics. Having been regarded as a rubber-stamping institution during the period of a single-party rule, parliament seemed to draw little academic interest. However, a few studies were done particularly on the relationship between the legislature and the executive as well as single-party parliamentary elections (Msekwa, 1978; Van Donge and Liviga, 1990; Okema, 1990). In most of these studies, the recurrent theme seemed to address the question of relative power between the parliament and the government, i.e., how much power did parliament have *vis-à-vis* government?

However, the 'parliament versus government' framework, as Gallagher *et al.*(1992) call it, does not seem to yield adequate leverage in an attempt to understand how parliaments that follow the majoritarian model work. After all, in a majoritarian model, members of the government are also members of the majority party in parliament. In this case, the government and parliament are literally one thing. In Tanzania, for instance, during the period of the single-party dominance, there had been no clear demarcation between the government and the parliament. Indeed, parliament was turned into a committee of the party used to rubber-stamp party policies and programmes. The one-party cabinet was constituted from this one-party parliament.

With the introduction of multiparty politics, parliament is still overwhelmingly controlled by one party, from which the cabinet is formed. It is, therefore, a majoritarian one-party cabinet. In this case, the 'parliament versus executive' framework is less likely to help us understand parliament's internal dynamics and processes. Thus, as Gallagher *et al.*(1992) suggest, rather than assessing the extent to which parliament controls or is controlled by the executive, it is useful to examine the performance of parliament in executing various roles so as to adequately capture the dynamics of the policy-making process inside parliament.

It should also be noted that the focus on the dynamics within parliament does not mean to understate the importance of parliamentary autonomy vis-à-vis the executive. The focus here is rather on how these internal processes and dynamics in parliament respond to the extent of autonomy at a given point in time.

However, measuring the performance of parliament might not be an easy task. Performance can be measured in several ways, i.e., in terms of the extent of parliament's representation, responsiveness to the wishes of the people, or the impact of enacted legislation on the larger population. This chapter assesses parliament's performance only in terms of its output from the legislative process. That is, what has parliament done in executing its various roles? By doing so, this chapter pays particular attention to what goes on inside parliament particularly on the politics of legislative process.

Furthermore, I regard legislators as independent political actors who seek to mould institutions to their own benefits. The relations among legislators, however, are largely shaped and informed by existing historical settings and institutional structures, which in turn tend to create a varied range of incentives that influence the behaviour of political actors. As Mainwaring (1993:198) points out, "Institutions create incentives and disincentives for political actors, shape actors' identities and establish the context in which policy-making occurs". It is in this regard that interactions among legislators will be analysed under the different settings in which they interact. There are three types of settings or modes, namely: an inter-party mode, in which relations between different actors in parliament and government are determined primarily by their respective party affiliations; a cross-party mode, in which ministers and members of parliament combine to interact on the basis of cross-party interests and an intra-party mode, in which relations between different actors in parliament and government are primarily determined by their affiliation to the same political party.

This chapter explores the performance of parliament in Tanzania in two consecutive periods; 1990-1995 and 1995-2000. The performance of the two parliaments will be assessed with respect to three sets of roles namely, in creating and sustaining governments, legislating and scrutinising the behaviour of governments (Gallagher *et al.*, 1992). These two parliaments varied in terms of the institutional rules that guided them and the nature of their composition. The 1990-1995 parliament was a single-party parliament, the last one of the 27–year single-party rule. In addition, while parliament tended to be a passive actor in influencing the policy-making process under a one-party regime, I would contend that in the 1990-1995 period, it exercised considerable influence on Tanzania's political system. The 1990-1995 period witnessed extensive institutional re-designing that transformed the old monolithic party system to pluralist democracy. Various laws were introduced in the country's constitution that among other things, enhanced the autonomy of parliament in the policy-making process.

The 1995-2000 parliament was the first parliament since 1965 to include opposition parties. The composition of the 1995-2000 parliament took a new form with members from Chama Cha Mapinduzi (CCM) (214), Civic United Front (CUF) (28), National Convention for Construction and Reform (NCCR-M) (19), Chama Cha Demokrasia na Maendeleo (CHADEMA) (4), and United Democratic Party (UDP) (4) United Republic of Tanzania (URT, 1997). Overall, opposition parties secured about 20 per cent of all parliamentary seats. Also, new rules under multiparty politics did introduce new categories of members into the 1995-2000 parliament. First, there was an increasing number of women as a result of a new rule that required 15 per cent of the total elected MPs to be women. As a result of this, the number of women MPs through special seats more than doubled from 15 in 1990 to 37 in the 1995 parliament (TEMCO, 2000). Indeed, this was the highest percentage of women MPs since independence. Second, the composition of members of parliament within CCM also changed significantly. The nominated seats of MPs were abolished. This, therefore, increased the number of directly elected MPs. Those removed from the list included 25 regional commissioners, 15 national members from mass organisations and 15 presidential nominees. Third, there was an addition of 52 new electoral constituencies that increased the number of parliamentary seats from 180 in 1990 to 232 in 1995 (URT, 1997)

In assessing the performance of these two parliaments, this chapter argues that relations among actors in the 1990-1995 parliament was largely determined by legislators' affiliation to the only political party, CCM. Hence, it was the intra-party mode that guided the behaviour of legislators. This mode created a set of compelling incentives for an intra-elite competition for policy influence and institutional autonomy.

The performance of the 1995-2000 parliament, on the other hand, was primarily determined by an inter-party mode in which the behaviour of both MPs and government ministers was largely influenced by their party affiliation. Through party discipline, party members were expected to support the party line on all important issues in parliament. Also, the locus of competition shifted from being intra-party to being inter-party. Thus, whereas in 1990-1995, members of parliament had an incentive to compete among themselves for policy influence as well as to maximise institutional (parliamentary) autonomy in the policy making process, in the 1995-2000 multi-party Parliament MPs and cabinet ministers from the majority party had incentives in designing institutional arrangements that would benefit their party.

Comparing performances of the 1990-1995 and 1995-2000 parliaments

There is one basic difference between the two parliaments. Whereas the former was under the single-party system, the latter was a multiparty institution. However, it is important to point out that unlike other single-party parliaments, the 1990-1995 Parliament operated in a different context due to several factors. First, the collapse of the Communist bloc in Eastern Europe and the demise of the former Soviet Union influenced the ruling party's way of running its own affairs. This was the time when the party had started to be more tolerant of dissent. Rather than being guided by a single ideology and unity of purpose, the party became more accommodative of diverse interests and demands and so was parliament. Secondly, and related to the above, was the existing disagreements over party's policies and principles within the governing elite. The disagreements were observed over the country's ideology, economic policies and the structure of the Union. This clash of interests within the ruling party created room for intensive debate in parliament. Thirdly was the liberalisation of the media industry which exposed a good deal of government misdeeds and scandals to the public and to the MPs. Unlike before, when the media was under the exclusive domain of the government, the independent media helped to make MPs better informed and therefore more critical of government actions.

Creating and sustaining the government

The 1990-1995 parliament
As stated above, the 1990-1995 parliament instituted several amendments to the constitution that transformed the old monolithic political system to a pluralist party system. For instance, from the legalisation of the multiparty system in 1992 to 1995, the 1977 constitution was amended six times in order to accommodate for new democratic changes. It is important to mention, however, that whereas these amendments were instituted by the single-party parliament of 1990-1995, they became politically effective with the beginning of the multiparty parliament in 1995. To a large extent, the 1990-1995 parliament was still functioning as a single-party legislature mainly guided by the intra-party mode.

The role of parliament in creating and sustaining government will be assessed by looking at two elements; the process of constituting the government and procedures for removing the government in case of the breach of the country's constitution. Before the establishment of the single-party system in 1965, the government had been constituted from the majority party parliament. This was a practice drawn from the 'Westminster style' of parliamentary system that Tanzania inherited at the time of independence in 1961. However, with the adoption of a *de-jure* one-party rule in 1965, the rule of party supremacy effectively took over, and it reduced parliament to a mere rubber-stamping institution.

The composition of parliament, therefore, shaped the character of the government. Cabinet ministers were drawn from both directly elected MPs and indirectly elected MPs, commonly referred to as nominated MPs. The latter category constituted about 30 per cent of the seats in the National Assembly, which included presidential-appointed candidates and nominees from mass organisations affiliated to the ruling party. The pool included 30 national members, 15 from the CCM women organisation and 15 from other mass organisations, 15 nominated members and 25 regional commissioners. Indeed, the probability of being appointed a minister was even higher for the nominated MPs compared to the elected MPs (Munishi, 1994). In 1990, for instance, 5 out of the 30, or 17 per cent of the national members of parliament were appointed as full cabinet ministers. Also, 4 out of 5, or 80 per cent of presidential-appointed members were appointed cabinet ministers. This is compared to only 16 out 179, or 9 per cent of elected MPs who were appointed cabinet ministers (Munishi, 1994) Thus, a system of having nominated MPs was a strategy of recruiting the governing elite. For instance, John Malecela was a nominated MP when he was appointed Prime Minister in early 1990s. Defending this system back in 1970, Nyerere said:

> 'I would add that one result of our [democratic] system is that individuals who have served the nation well are sometimes not elected, even when the United Republic [of Tanzania] could still benefit from their services in parliament or government.... In the exceptional case of an overriding national need for the services of a person who is not elected, the President has the necessary powers'. (Nyerere, 1970).

The representativeness of the government was somehow limited due to the presence of a significant number of indirectly elected members of parliament. In a study done by Kjekshus about the 1970 parliament, it was established that on the average the elected (constituency) MP proved to be active in raising various policy issues than the nominated or national MP. The extent of activism was measured in terms of interventions made and the number of questions asked by an individual MP in parliamentary meetings (Kjekshus, 1974).

Furthermore, parliament's power to oversee the government was also legally constrained. During the single-party era, the constitution allowed the president to dissolve parliament at any time. This tended to limit parliament's power to discipline the government. Also, the president was totally immune from criminal and civil proceedings for those acts committed in his/her capacity as president. In addition, parliament had no power to exercise a 'vote of no confidence' against the prime minister. In other words, once the government was constituted, there was very little that parliament could do to get it out of power.

The 1995-2000 parliament
With the advent of multiparty politics, role of parliament in creating and sustaining government has changed. The process of institutional designing has attempted to make Tanzania's multiparty system closer to the parliamentary system in which executive power is concentrated in the hands of the majority party. In this system, the executive basically remained a one-party cabinet.

The composition of the 1995-2000 parliament seemed to have affected the character of the government in terms of its extent of representativeness. All ex-officio MPs, such as regional commissioners, presidential-nominated MPs as well as members from mass organisations, were eliminated from the list. Also, unlike before when the prime minister could be appointed from indirectly elected MPs, the new law requires the president to appoint the prime minister from a pool of directly elected MPs only belonging to the majority party in parliament. This system has to a certain extent shifted the locus of elite competition within the ruling party from intra-elite competition to elite competition at the constituency level.

With regards to the termination or removal of the government in case of breaching of the country's constitution, Act. No. 20 of 1992 empowers the legislature to impeach the president if he/she is found guilty of violating the constitution of the United Republic. The president can be removed if a two-thirds majority of parliament passes a resolution calling for this move. Also, unlike before, upon leaving office the president is not immune from criminal and civil proceedings if found guilty by impeachment. The same procedures can be applied to impeach the vice-president in case of the breach of the constitution. In addition, the Nineth Amendment empowers parliament to approve or disapprove a presidential appointee for the office of the prime minister.

Also, parliament can dismiss the government by passing a vote of no confidence in the prime minister. The vice-president is now elected with the president as his/her 'running mate' and not appointed by the presidential victor.

Furthermore, parliament's position to sustain the government is enhanced by the new law that limits the president's power to dissolve parliament. Unlike before when the president could dissolve parliament at any time, this power is now defined in a more precise way. The new law states that the president can only dissolve parliament under specific conditions: 1) when parliament refuses to pass the annual budget proposed by the government; 2) when the government is defeated on an important bill; 3) when the government loses its majority support in parliament; 4) when its lifetime of five years has expired; 5) at any time within the last 12 months of its lifetime, unless the speaker of the National Assembly has received a special request to establish an impeachment process.

Legislating (policy making role)

Parliaments play a critical role as law making institutions. In Tanzania, the 1977 constitution empowers parliament to enact new legislations and amend the constitution. This is provided in Article 98 of the Union constitution. Article 98 (1) states that amending any provision in the constitution requires two-thirds majority of all the MPs. However, as stated in paragraph (b) of the same sub-article, where these alterations touch matters of the Union, a two-thirds majority of MPs from each part of the Union must be achieved.

The 1990-1995 Parliament

There are marked variations between the two parliaments in terms of the implications of the laws enacted. Under the Intra-Party Parliament of 1990-1995, the move was towards greater legislative independence in relation to the executive. This inclination toward greater legislative independence goes back to mid 1980s. As stated above, the three decades of the single-party rule in Tanzania led to an omnipotent presidency at the expense of the National Assembly. However, beginning mid 1980s there emerged some slight changes, which intended to increase the role of parliament in the policy making process rather than making it a mere rubber stamping organ. The reason behind this change is beyond the scope of the chapter but just briefly, the following seem to be contributing factors: the adoption of liberal-market policies, which in turn introduced a new context for policy debates and policy implementation; and the move towards the separation of executive powers between the presidency and party chairmanship in mid 1980s. A clash of interests between the two centres of power (i.e. the president and the CCM chairman) translated into the struggle for institutional designing in order to influence political and economic trends in the country. In so doing, Nyerere seemed to be keenly interested in counter-checking the power of the presidency by enhancing that of parliament. For instance, following the Fourth Constitutional Amendment Act of 1984, the presidential term was limited to two terms, five years each.

Thus, the 1990-1995 Parliament emerged out of the pre-1990 political and economic realities. The legislators had an incentive to check the strong presidency and maximise their sphere of influence within the intra-party political setting. This is manifested by a number of amendments cited above, for example, parliament's power to have a vote of no confidence in the prime minister, to impeach the president, and to set some specific conditions on the president's power to dissolve parliament.

Furthermore, the 1990-1995 single-party parliament introduced historical changes in the country's constitution that transparent the political system from a single-party system to a multiparty system.. The first significant constitutional change was provided in the Eighth Amendment of 1992 that abolished one-party rule and introduced a multiparty system. The famous section 3, (1), of the 1977 Constitution, which provided for the establishment of a one-party state, was repealed and replaced by a statement indicating that Tanzania is a democratic multiparty state. Also, two other important articles were removed from the constitution; article 3, (2-3), and article 10 which provided for the supremacy of the sole party in governing the country. Instead, provisions that give supremacy to the constitution and parliament as a law making institution were instituted. This was followed by a series of constitutional amendments covering such issues as electoral rules and regulations, executive-legislative relations, the judicial system and the rule of law. Moreover, other rules to liberalise the political system were introduced by the same parliament before the formal introduction of the multiparty politics. These included the amendment in the Cooperative Societies Act (1991) that provided for the establishment of an autonomous cooperative society, as well as a provision that established an apex semi-autonomous organization for trade unions, the Organisation of Tanzania's Trade Union (OTTU).

With the adoption of the Political Parties Act, many opposition groups were formed. By July 1992, 43 opposition groups had picked up registration application forms from the registrar's office (Mmuya and Chaligha, 1992). However, only 13 political parties were able to meet the prescribed conditions and secure full registration.

What can be said about the new rules is that they were generally intended to liberalise the political system without necessarily fully democratising it. To a large extent, the whole political transition process was a result of a careful strategy by the ruling party to introduce plural politics without losing the grip on power. In so doing, some of the instituted rules work very much in favour of the ruling party. Nevertheless, the point remains that rules enacted by this parliament were geared toward not only greater legislative independence but also towards a certain degree of political liberalisation.

The 1995-2000 parliament

The 1995 first multiparty elections changed the rules of the game. Unlike in the single-party parliament, interactions among legislative actors in the 1995-2000 Parliament were primarily guided by an inter-party mode in which an MP's party affiliation comes first before anything else. While the survey data presented by Mallya's chapter in this book show that the MPs are first accountable to the voters, inside parliament, voters' needs and demands are translated into policies or laws by the party machinery. Thus, in order to serve their voters, which in turn would ensure their electoral success, MPs from the majority party have an incentive to ensure that their bills are approved. As Msekwa (1996:75-76) categorically states:

> 'Under multi-partism [sic], a serious defeat in parliament may cause the removal of the government from office... Naturally, the winning party wants to retain its prize for that whole five years of parliament.

For that reason they [MPs of the winning party] will strive to avoid doing anything which might bring about the loss of that precious prize before the end of their term.'

It is from this rationale that the 1995-2000 institutional re-designing such a strong presidency and majoritarian forms of legislative representation was geared more towards benefiting the dominant party. Some of the rules enacted were intended to achieve these goals. For instance, in order to ensure a presidential electoral victory for the incumbent party, the constitution was amended to introduce a simple majority rule for the presidential victor as opposed to the previous rule which required an absolute majority. The same constitutional amendments empowered the president to appoint up to 10 members of parliament to join the majority party in parliament. According to article 66(1) of the 1977 Constitution as amended, these appointees need not to be members of any political party and may be chosen for their expertise or their social standing the National Executive Committee (NEC, 2000). It has to be recalled that the 1990-1995 parliament did enact a law that actually abolished the power of the president to appoint MPs.

Thus, whereas the 1990-1995 parliament took away some executive powers in an attempt to improve parliamentary autonomy, the 1995-2000 Parliament seemed to be giving the powers back in order to maximise the party's electoral and policy success under the competitive political system.

Scrutinising the government

Parliaments are supposed to play a role of overseeing government performance. Various methods are used in scrutinising the performance of the government, including the 'question period,' which gives MPs an opportunity to submit questions to ministers that must be answered within a fixed time. In addition, parliamentary debates on each individual ministry during annual budget session provide a room for parliamentary scrutiny. The committee system is another mechanism of overseeing the work of the Government. In Tanzania there are 13 standing committees serving three main areas namely, economic and finance sector, legal and constitution affairs sector and social sector. While they cannot change bills, these committees are supposed to discuss and deliberate on various issues under their jurisdiction before they are sent to the National Assembly. In this way, committees can give suggestions, which are subject to approval by the minister concerned before they are presented to parliament for debate. Apart from standing committees, there are probe committees temporarily constituted to investigate specific matters. The probe committee ceases to exist after tabling its report to the House.

While parliament's role in overseeing the government has been practiced in both parliaments under study, the extent of control exercised by the parliament over the government has been largely affected by the corresponding party mode.

The 1990-1995 Parliament

The intra-party mode that characterised the 1990-1995 Parliament tended to create incentives for parliamentarians to regard themselves largely as individuals within a one-party political setting. However, it is important to point out that throughout the single-party period, the behaviour of MPs was largely influenced by the extent of party control and supervision. Any kind of opposition to the party's policies and principles was, in most cases, severely discouraged by the party top organs. As already mentioned elsewhere in this volume, in 1968, the National Executive Committee (NEC) of the party expelled seven outspoken MPs from the party, and therefore from parliament, 'for having grossly violated the party creed, both in their attitudes and actions, and for showing very clear opposition to the party and its policies.' (Msekwa, 1978:48). Similarly, in 1989 the NEC expelled four top party officials from Zanzibar, including the then chief minister, for allegedly causing political disturbances in Zanzibar. The officials were questioning anomalies in the Constitution of the United Republic of Tanzania. Thus, the expulsion of dissidents was one of the most common techniques used to deal with the most outspoken and critical MPs.

However, as stated above, the 1990-1995 Parliament operated under a different context. The most important factor was the adoption of multiparty politics in July 1992. Rather than resorting to old techniques of dealing with dissidents, the new technique was to co-opt the most critical MPs by giving them top government posts as a way of silencing them. This was intentionally pursued in order to prevent defections from the ruling party to the newly established opposition parties.

Thus, the 1990-1995 parliament provided a great opportunity for MPs to be themselves and to pursue their private agenda without the fear of either being expelled from the party or facing defeat of bills in a single-party parliament. It is in this context that the 1990-1995 Parliament was relatively lively in terms of parliamentary debates and very critical of government policies and programmes.

One of the major issues that created a hot debate in parliament was the question of the nature of the Union between Tanganyika and Zanzibar. On various occasions, the government was challenged to provide answers to issues that used to be 'sensitive' and therefore immune to parliamentary or public scrutiny.

The controversial entry of Zanzibar to the Organisation of Islamic Community (OIC) in December 1992, was one case in point. The issue was first reported by a privately owned newspaper, *Motomoto*, before it was picked up by parliament. At first the government denied the report as mere allegations with no grain of truth. After an extensive debate in parliament, led by the parliament's Constitutional and Legal Affairs Committee, it was established that the Zanzibar government had grossly violated the Union Constitution which puts all foreign affairs under the Union government's jurisdiction. As a result of this pressure, the government was compelled to admit that Zanzibar's unilateral entry to the OIC was indeed unconstitutional and it was forced to pull out of the organisation. Following this, Zanzibar's membership was eventually abrogated by the OIC.

Furthermore, the structure of the Union was another issue of debate in parliament, which almost threatened the survival of the Union itself. Other interested actors aside, the Presidential Commission on Party Systems in Tanzania (the Nyalali Commission) had recommended the need to restructure the existing Union by introducing a federal arrangement of governments. According to the 1964 Articles of Union and Acts of Union, the Union is structured under a two-government system. This includes the Union government with exclusive power and authority in and for Tanganyika in all matters and over Union matters in Zanzibar and the Zanzibar government with exclusive powers and authority over all non-Union matters in Zanzibar (Shivji, 1990; Makaramba, 1997).

The parliamentary debate was preoccupied with four major issues namely, matters relating to power allocation between the two parts of the Union; matters relating to financial arrangements (who is to get what, how and at what cost); matters relating to perceptions of unequal benefits and matters relating to violation of the Union constitution and anomalies in the constitution (TEMCO, 1997) All these issues in totality led to the demand for the creation of a Tanganyika government within a Union structure. A group of 55 MPs, commonly referred to as the G55, signed a private members' bill demanding for a separate Tanganyika government, which with exclusive power and authority over all non-Union matters in Tanganyika. This motion was contrary to the government's policy of maintaining a two-government structure as established in the 1964 Articles of the Union.

The government was able to hijack the issue by passing a motion that arrangements would be made in order to involve the public to give their views on the best type of structure of the Union. With the advent of multiparty politics, the question of the structure of the Union is more of the agenda of opposition parties. Meanwhile, in the course of silencing the issue, the government resorted to co-optation strategy by offering ministerial posts to the most outspoken MPs. For instance, Hon. Phillip Marmo, who was the chair of Constitutional and Legal Affairs Committee during the OIC issue, was later appointed Minister for Information; Hon. Njelu Kasaka, the leader of the G55, was made Deputy Minister in the Ministry for Agriculture.

During the 1990-1995 Parliament, three private members' bills were introduced in the House, namely: The G55 motion on the formation of the government of Tanganyika; Hon. Patrick Qorro's private member's bill on the need to form a commission to investigate the safety of environment of natural game reserves and Hon. Jared Gachocha's motion demanding that the government should form a commission to investigate the effect of refugees from Rwanda and Burundi on Ngara and Karagwe districts.

The 1995-2000 Parliament

Unlike the 1990-1995 Parliament, the first multiparty Parliament of 1995-2000 was seen to be lacking the rigour and the drama of the previous parliament. Some of the newspapers carried title such as "Is our parliament losing its esteemed prestige and dignity? (Msekwa, 2000:73) Parliamentary debates were seen to be dull and boring with lack of critical analysis and automatic approval of legislations. Indeed, to some people, the 1995-2000 Parliament was a vivid sign of parliamentary decay and decline. The statistics also supported this widely held view. Whereas the 1990-1995 had three private members' bills (which are hard to come by in most majoritarian parliaments), the 1995-2000 Parliament had none.

This observed pattern is largely a function of the inter-party mode of parliamentary interactions. As stated earlier, the adoption of multiparty politics has created a different setting that in turn shapes the behaviour of MPs differently. In this mode, it is argued, 'individual parliamentarians think of themselves first and foremost as members of their party's parliamentary group rather than as individual members' (Ghallagher, 1992:83). This is enhanced by the principle of party discipline in which MPs are expected to vote along party lines, particularly on a three-line party whip.

In addition, under the inter-party mode brought about by the introduction of the multiparty system, the government is compelled to act differently. That is, trying as much as possible not to table bills that would negatively affect the party's chance for re-election. As Pius Msekwa argues, in order to ensure its survival in office, 'the government proposals are of necessity prepared very carefully, thereby leaving no opportunity for a 'vigorous' challenge from other parliamentarians, including the opposition camp.' In so doing, Msekwa (2000:78) concludes, 'expectations of parliamentary 'vigorous challenges' to government proposals [under multiparty politics] are largely misplaced.' In this case, obeying the law of anticipated reactions, the government might have made sure that it did not submit any unpopular proposals.

There are ways of detecting dissenting views over a certain bill. Before being tabled for a whole House debate, bills are first sent to relevant committees for discussion. At the party level, the discussions are conducted under the party caucuses. In this way, frontbenchers can accommodate the views of the majority backbenchers well in advance before the whole House debate. Thus, the passing of legislation without the so-called 'vigorous challenge' effect resulted in may party cohesion and legitimacy rather than passivity among the backbenchers. An example can be cited to support this pattern. In 1998, the CCM backbenchers rejected a government bill called 'the Government Pension Act, 1998.' The majority of the MPs had expressed their reservations on a particular clause of the bill that intended to increase the retirement age from 55 years to 60 years. The bill faced some resistance in the Constitutional and Legal Affairs Committee, chaired by the Hon. Arcado Ntagazwa. Moreover, the CCM's caucus intensively challenged the bill. In any case, when the government moved the bill to the whole House for debate, it lost. While the defeat of the bill was also explained by the fact that MPs' benefits were not taken into account, the 'CCM parliamentary back bench rebellion of November 1998,' is an example of what happens when the front benchers ignore the views of the majority backbenchers.

Conclusion

The discussion above has attempted to demonstrate the effect of a party mode in influencing the performance of parliament in creating and sustaining governments, legislating, and scrutinising the actions of governments. The findings presented have shown that the two parliaments performed differently largely due to the fact that the 1990-1995 parliament was mainly guided by the intra-party mode and therefore, created a great opportunity for inclination towards institutional autonomy and pluralism. It was the inter-party mode that guided the 1995-2000 parliament and therefore, shifted its focus towards preservation of power under the pluralist competitive politics.

References

Gallagher, M., Laver, M. and Main, P. (1992). *Representative Governments in Modern Europe: Institutions, Parties and Governments*, New York: McGraw-Hill

Kjekshus, H. (1974). Perspectives on the Second Parliament in Election Study Committee(ed), *Socialism and Participation: Tanzania 1970 Elections*.

Mainwaring, S. (1993). 'Presidentialism, Multipartism and Democracy: the difficult combination' *Comparative Political Studies*. Vol.26 no. 2.

Makaramba, R. (1997). *A New Constitutional Order for Tanzania? Why and How*, Dar es Salaam: Friedrich Ebert Stiftung.

Mmuya, M and Chaligha, A. (1992). *Towards Multi-party Politics in Tanzania*, Dar es Salaam, Dar es Salaam University Press.

Msekwa, P. (1978). *Towards Party Supremacy*, Dar es Salaam: Dar es salaam University Press.

Msekwa, P. (1996). *Reflections on Tanzania's First Multi-party parliament: 1995-2000*, Dar es Salaam: Dar es Salaam University Press.

Munishi, G. K. (1994). "What election results reveal and what they cannot expose" in Mukandala, R. and Othman, H. (eds), *Liberalization and Politics: the 1990 Elections in Tanzania*, Dar es Salaam: Dar es Salaam University Press.

National Electoral Commission (2000). *A Handbook of Tanzania Electoral Laws and Regulations*. Dar es Salaam: NEC

Nyerere, G. K. (1970). *Arusha Declaration Parliament, 1965-1970*. Dar es salaam: Government Printer.

Okema, M. (1990)."Some Salient Changes in the Tanzanian Parliamentary System" in Othman, H., Bavu, I. and Okema, M. (eds) *Tanzania: Democracy in Transition*. Dar es Salaam: Dar es Salaam University Press.

Shivji, I. (1990). "The Legal Foundations of the Union in Tanzania's Union and Zanzibar Constitutions", Professorial Inaugural Lecture, University of Dar es Salaam.

TEMCO (2000). *The 2000 General Elections in Tanzania*.

TEMCO (1997). *The 1995 General Elections in Tanzania.*

United Republic of Tanzania (1997). *The Report of the National Electoral Commission on the 1995 Presidential and Parliamentary Elections*, Dar es Salaam: Government Printer.

Van Donge, J.K and Liviga, A. (1990). "The 1985 Parliamentary Elections: a conservative election" in Othman, H. Bavu, I and Okema, M. (eds), *Tanzania: Democracy in Transition*, Dar es Salaam, Dar es Salaam University Press.

Index

Analysis: *See* historical analysis
    See also theoretical analysis
Accountability: *See* representation models
    See also role of MPs

Budgetary process 2

Civic rights 4
Choice of clusters 8
See also methodology
Cohesion – solidarity see models 39

Constitution 1-4
– changes 65-66
– amendments 68

Committee
– consultations 163-164, 161, 172
– powers 162
– timing 163
– recommendations

Controversies. *See* role of MPs
Competence of MPs. *See* performance
Constraints to democracy 47

Data processing 18
Data analysis 18
Democracy 25, 28. *See also* Tanzania representation
Decentralisation 36, 38
Decision making 177. *See also* role of MPs

Economic variables 34.
See also representation
Election manifestos
See representation models

Freedom – civil organisation 34.
See also representation

Election manifestos. *See* representation models

Freedom – civil organisation 36
See also representation
Features – representation 41
Government
– Politics 27
– Control of representatives 36
See also representation

Historical analysis 25-45
See also theoretical analysis

Instruments 13. *See also* methodology
Interim Constitution – Parliament 56

Liberal democracies. *See* democracy
LEGCO 46, 47
Liberal democracy
– Theory 114-117
– Lobbying – Parliament 134-138
– Process 138-142

Multiparty system 4, 68-71, 78
Multiparty democracy 78-80
See also political systems
Multiparty parliament 184-198
See also parliament
Members of Parliament
– Roles 4
– Survey. *See* methodology
– Parliament 49
– Work environment 73
– Socio political 82
– Voter's support 84, 129-130, 167
– NGO support 85, 130-132
– Reasons for contesting 86
– Powers and authority 87, 88
– Finance 88, 89
– Motivation 96-101
– Adherence 102-111, 167

- Relationship with parties 122-126
- Relations with government 126-129
- Political competence 167
- Elections 167
- Survey. *See* methodology

Multiparty politics 167
Methodology 7-24
Model
- Parliament 49

National Assembly. *See* Parliament

Organisation – campaigns. *See* models
Opposition party – controversies 169.
See role of MPs

Parliament 1, 2, 50
- Sovereignty 48
- Independence Constitution 49
- Dissolution 49
- Power encroachment 60
- Composition 62
- Role 188-199
- Powers 62
- Decline 63
- Lobbying 143
- Performance 185-198
- Forms 143-160

Performance of MPs 173-183. *See also* role of MPs.
Procedure changes 160
Principles of representation 93
Political system. *See* Tanzania
Power of Privilege Act 2
Problems faced 18. *See also* methodology, political theories 26, 114
Political culture 33.
See also representation
Party control – representatives 36
Partisanship. *See* models
Party solidarity. *See* models

Questionnaire design 14, 15
See also methodology
Quality of data 19

REDET 7-8. *See also* methodology
Representatives 117-119, 167
Representation 25
- Historical perspective 25-44
- Models 25, 34-40
- Functions 25, 30, 42-44
- Theories 25-27
- Principles 28, 29, 30
- Factors 30-32
- Role of MPs 168-183
- Principles 28
- Criticisms 47
- Views of MPs 179-183

Representative government 28, 117-119
Republican Constitution 52-56
Remuneration of MPs 171

Single party 4
Sample survey design 7. *See* methodology
Sampling design 9
Survey methodology 13
Sampling errors 20
Superimposition 27
Socialism 58, 59
Single party parliament 184

Tabulation of findings 21-24
Theoretical analysis 25-45
See also historical analysis

Tanzania
- Parliament 46, 182-183, 186-198
- Pre-independence 36, 119
- Colonialism 46
- Political system 75, 184-198
- Political parties 113
- Administrative culture 171
- Legislative Council 119
- Elections (1965-1990), 119-122, 184

Voters
- Control of representatives. *See also* representatives
- Rights 167-183

Women MPs p. 170

www.ingramcontent.com/pod-product-compliance
Lightning Source LLC
Chambersburg PA
CBHW051523230426
43668CB00012B/1720